THE GOD WHO CHANGES LIVES

The God Who Changes Lives

Edited by Mark Elsdon-Dew

HTB PUBLICATIONS

LONDON

ISBN 1 898838 03 8

Front cover and text illustrations by Charlie Mackesy.

Editor's acknowledgements

I owe a huge debt of gratitude to this book's contributors, who
not only gave several hours of their time in interviews and
amending the manuscript, but have opened up parts of their lives
where they were often at their most vulnerable.
I would also like to thank Gil Rea and Bridget Fletcher for all
their help with preparing the final manuscript.

Designed and produced by Bookprint Creative Services
P.O. Box 827, BN21 3YJ, England for
HTB PUBLICATIONS
Brompton Road, London, SW7 1JA.
Printed in Great Britain.

Contents

"Write down for the coming generation what the Lord has done, so that people not yet born will praise him."

Psalm 102 v 18

Alpha

Many of the contributors to this book make reference to the *Alpha* course, a practical introduction to the Christian faith which has had a remarkable impact on many people's lives. The course, which runs on 10 consecutive Wednesday evenings (or mornings) at Holy Trinity Brompton, has proved so popular that it is now running in more than 2,000 other churches across Britain and now, increasingly, around the world.

Foreword

by Sandy Millar
Vicar of Holy Trinity Brompton

It is immensely refreshing and encouraging to hear of real life stories of everyday men and women to whom God has come alive and whom he has touched in such different ways. For the same God who came to earth as Jesus Christ 2,000 years ago is still at work today bringing forgiveness, healing, restoration and, perhaps above all, new hope and faith.

Many of the people who describe what happened to them in this book have been affected by an Alpha course – the single most effective means of looking into the Christian faith that I know.

Hundreds of people all over the country and now increasingly all over the world, are taking the opportunity to find out more about God through Alpha courses and there's almost certainly one running somewhere near you.

If these stories encourage you to look for faith in this living God or strengthen you further in the faith you have, they will in themselves make the publication of this book worthwhile.

Introduction

by Mark Elsdon-Dew

The stories in this book are almost all the results of interviews I conducted with members of the congregation of Holy Trinity Brompton, a large Anglican church in central London, during the past four years. They were published on the back page of the church's monthly newspaper *HTB in Focus* under the title 'Holy Ghost Stories', where they have attracted a wide following.

Many are stories about how people came to faith in Jesus Christ but there are also accounts of healings, answers to prayer, and 'coincidences' which bear the hallmarks of God. Some are simply testimonies of the presence of God in situations which might otherwise be periods of despair in people's lives.

My barometer in deciding whether to include a story has always depended upon two questions:

1. Is the person telling the story someone whose current lifestyle is such that I can trust their account – and who is not so new to the Christian life that they are liable to be rocked by the very act of telling their story publicly?

2. Is this story unusual enough – yet 'real' enough –

to prompt the reader to accept that *something* unusual took place, which could possibly be put down to the presence of the living God?

It is an amazing privilege to be a journalist working in a growing, living, vibrant church where there is a dependence upon God to do what only he can do. It means that amazing events are happening all the time.

But we are just one church in one city – and similar stories of God at work can be found in thousands of churches all over the country. There is nothing special about our church. It is the unique God we worship who is special.

Each of the contributors to this book can, in their own way, echo the words of Simon Peter in his letter at the end of the New Testament: "We have not depended on made-up stories in making known to you the mighty coming of our Lord Jesus Christ. With our own eyes we saw his greatness."

"He pulled me out of the deep waters."
Psalm 18:16

1

"I went up to my bedroom with this terrible pain ...
I screamed, 'Oh God, if you're there, do something!'"

The story of Deirdre Hurst

*David and Deirdre Hurst celebrated their Silver
Wedding anniversary with a special service at Holy
Trinity Brompton in 1995. Here Deirdre tells the
story of how she and David became Christians in
desperate circumstances 15 years ago:*

I was brought up in a devout Roman Catholic
household with church every Sunday. I went to a
convent at the age of four and a half. We were always
going to church and there was a chapel in the convent
where we seemed to spend an awful lot of our time from
a very, very early age. To me, my religion meant a great
fear of God. I was terrified of him and terrified of doing
anything wrong. I kept the letter of the law, the Holy
Days of Obligation – everything.

When I left school I got a job as a secretary in a

theatrical agency in the West End. So at the age of 19, I entered this extremely glamorous world. We represented huge stars – Peter Sellers, Roger Moore and others. But I could no longer keep on doing all those things to please God. So shortly after my 21st birthday, I said "Right God. I am sorry. Good-bye." I had to keep up something for my parents so I did go to church at Christmas, but otherwise I just totally shut off from God.

By this time I'd moved to work in films. I worked for Sam Spiegel and was production assistant for something called Horizon Pictures which was Sam Spiegel's London company. We were living in the glory of *Lawrence of Arabia* and all the other films that he'd made and that was tremendously exciting. I couldn't wait to get to work. I just adored it and was usually seconded to some other famous producers to work for them, so it was a terribly exciting life.

I was coming up to 25 and I was desperate to be married. A friend of mine had been to a medium and she suggested that I should go. I went to see this woman and she was very, very sweet and she started to give me confidence by describing exactly where I had been the day before. I had been to New College, Oxford, with a friend and this woman described exactly this arch at New College, Oxford. I couldn't believe it. Then she proceeded to tell me that in September of that year I'd get a telephone call offering me a tremendous job and that I was to take that job because my destiny was in it. She also saw that I would be married one day. That was all I went there to hear.

In September that year a telephone call came. It was a man called Jo Durden-Smith. Lord Bernstein had given him and some other producers carte blanche to do specials in London and to form a team around him. So he rang me to offer me a 13-week contract and a sum of money which was unbelievable as far as I was concerned. I don't think I would have left Sam Spiegel if it had not been for the medium, but because of this medium I said yes. So I went to join Granada.

So I went to work at Granada as a researcher and I honestly thought I couldn't be happier. These people I was working with were terribly bright – all Oxbridge graduates – and I used to mug up on philosophers by buying the *New York Review of Books* which would review books about the philosophers.

The following year I met David at a lunch party and one of the first things he asked me was whether I had ever heard of Ludwig Wittgenstein, who was a philosopher. As it happened, I had just been reading an article about him in the *New York Review of Books*. Unknown to me, David had a list of things which were his criteria for any girl he would think of marrying – and one of them was that she would have heard of Wittgenstein. David asked me back to his house for a drink after the lunch party and there was all the rock music that I was into – The Doors, Janice Joplin, The Grateful Dead, The Stones... David had records of them already. By my standards, David was very straight. He had got a scholarship to Oxford, was very bright, and a chartered accountant. But of course it worked absolutely tremendously. We got married in May 1970. David had inherited some money at the time, so we bought a house in Westminster. He had just started a job in the Strategy Department of the *Sunday Times*, so he was being very successful.

I was so happy I couldn't believe it. I had this man I absolutely adored, this wonderful house, all these really trendy friends and quite a lot of money. We used to do things like spend three weeks in Greece and drive across the Channel and do gastronomic tours of Normandy. If we felt like it, we'd do it.

But we were doing things which we now know didn't please the Lord. We were conducting Tarot sessions in our house. We didn't know it was wrong then of course. David was fascinated by it and he used to read the cards with terrible accuracy. We were also passionately interested in astrology and we would watch what personalities people were. That fascinated me really.

Suddenly things began to go very wrong. I began to drink very seriously and had to be dried out in a clinic. The drinking partly started at Granada because it was a very 'drink lifestyle'. People would come in with bottles of wine in the morning. I always loved the taste of wine. Most of those people around that table did not become alcoholics, but I was the one it affected.

David and I used to spend a lot of money on drink and used to give huge parties, hiring catering staff to help pass around the canapés and the champagne. I began to drink very, very heavily because my body began to crave the alcohol. David was a heavy drinker and it probably didn't dawn on him for a year or so that actually I was craving it during the day. In 1972, which was the property boom, we sold our house in Westminster and bought a five-storey house in Alexander Street. I then went into a clinic in 1973 and was dried-out from alcoholism and began to become very depressed.

Somebody said all my problems would be solved if I had a baby so we thought we'd have a baby. Lucy was born in October 1974 and it was wonderful. But although I was very happy, I was still so terribly depressed. And then, for the next seven or eight years, came a series of these clinics and mental homes for this unbelievable depression. Sometimes I just could not operate at all. I couldn't get out of bed or anything. It wasn't the drink because I had stopped drinking. I was just terribly ill. I couldn't work. I couldn't do anything. So Lucy's early years involved my mother-in-law helping out and taking her away and hiring a nanny. Then Lucy would come back to London if I had come out of a clinic.

David was in a terrible state because all the money had just disappeared. We lost a lot of money in the property crash and our house in Alexander Street wasn't worth what we had paid for it. I couldn't bear the fact that David hadn't got any more money. I just couldn't bear it. Very often I was too ill to manage the house and I used to be taken away and put in places over a long period. This went on for absolutely ages.

I was on an incredible amount of legal drugs, but I would shake violently all the time. We had to sell that house in 1977. We sold it very poorly. And at this time I had a brief respite from this illness. I can remember one day sitting on the bed and I remember clenching my fist and saying: "I am going to get better. I am going to be normal. I'm not going to take all these pills any more. I'm going to be normal." And I remember taking all the pills and flushing them all down the loo and, by force of will, it made a difference.

I went out and found this fabulous little cottage off Duke's Lane, W8 and we moved there and lived there. I was roughly all right for about a year until 1978. I had about a year's respite where I just gripped my palms and said, "Right, I am going to be well."

Then in 1979 we moved to Earl's Court and I became really ill again. I thought I might as well be dead. I can't tell you what it's like. It's like you're going mad. David would have to rush home. Then I would usually have sleep treatment for three weeks, when they would just knock me out. David was paying for these clinics and my parents sometimes did too. It was just unbelievable – completely dehumanising.

David had remembered that we knew one girl who was a Christian. He remembered that she had asked God for a car and that we were absolutely shocked that you could ask God for anything like that. Anyway, he thought he'd ask her to help. So in 1980 we went to Suffolk to stay with the girl, whose name was Serena Campbell Lambert. She was shocked to see me because she hadn't seen me since Lucy was young and I was shaking so much. You can't disguise it you see. She said: "I'd love to pray for you but I haven't got the power. But I know people who have and we will pray and fast and my group will pray and fast to see where you should be sent."

I had always loved my food and the idea that anyone would actually give up food for me..... it sort of touched my hardened heart somehow. I thought it was unbelievable that any group of people that I didn't know would actually give up food for me. So we were sent to see Richard and Joyce Connor. Joyce was a charismatic Catholic and Richard a charismatic Anglican. I spent three hours telling Joyce my story. At the end, I expected her to say, "Oh you poor girl. Oh that's absolutely terrible." But instead she said "Poor David". I was absolutely furious.

David had been with Richard all day and I had been with Joyce and at the end Richard said, "Right, now we're going to open the Bible and I am going to ask you if you want Jesus Christ to come into your lives." Well, of course I'd never heard anything like that before in my life, and to my utter astonishment David said "Yes". He would like to give his life to Christ. They then turned to me and said, "Would you like to give your life to Christ?" And I said, "I'm not going to do that because you'll send me back to the Catholic Church." I knew I couldn't do all those laws any more.

From that moment David was a committed Christian. Three weeks later somebody rang and said that Joyce Connor had suggested that she get in touch. She invited us to something at Holy Trinity Brompton on a Tuesday evening. It was July 1980 and there was a joint home group in Church House with Charlie Colchester leading it. Later, we went to Sandy Millar's Bible study group. At the time, he was a curate living in St Paul's House. I thought they were all absolutely mad, but I honestly wanted to seek God because I knew nothing else had helped me and I thought this might.

In 1981 I became pregnant and then lost the baby at around four-and-a-half months. On the morning of July 10, 1981, having had a D & C – the operation women have after they've had miscarriages – I was absolutely desperate. I went up to my bedroom with this terrible pain and I slammed myself down on the bed. I screamed, "Oh God! If you're there, do something." And at that moment he walked into my room by his Spirit. I had the most powerful manifestation of God in that bedroom. Love came down into my life and I saw that Jesus died for me. I saw his love for me, and in that one fell swoop I fell in love with Jesus. I remember there was a total surrender of my whole life to him. There were things I had to give up – like my obsession with make-up and hair, gold bangles and things like that. I was converted in the most powerful, powerful way. It was just unbelievable. I must have been up there in my room for about four hours. I was just lost in God.

That morning, a package had been delivered filled with foam packaging. And when I came downstairs, there was my five-year-old sitting still, happily playing with it. It was as if angels were playing with her. She was being looked after and protected, just playing with these boxes while all this was going on in the bedroom. I phoned Serena Campbell Lambert, the woman who had started the ball rolling with her prayer and fasting group. I talked and talked and talked. Then I had a week walking around with this total love of Jesus. I mean I was really well, though I was still smoking 60 cigarettes a day.

Suddenly after about a week it was like war broke out in my mind. Sandy had asked us to learn Scriptures in his Bible study group and these Scriptures came back. Suddenly the Scripture I needed was 1 Corinthians 10 v 13 – that God would not allow us to be tempted beyond that which we are able to bear but would give the way of escape. That came to mind and I spoke that out against the Enemy and asked him to leave in the name of Jesus. After four days of this war the Enemy just left me and the war stopped.

I still needed healing from the miscarriage because I was still having a lot of pain so I went to Holy Trinity Brompton to a healing service on the Wednesday. It was quite funny actually. There was some sort of 'famous healer' who was supposed to come to pray for the sick and Patrick Whitworth [then HTB curate] was going to do the Communion. But the 'famous healer' didn't turn up and so after the Communion Patrick said, "I am terribly sorry but so and so hasn't arrived and so you're lumbered with me. Will you come up for prayer?" And I went up there and asked Patrick to pray for the miscarriage and various sorts of things, and he laid hands on me. He hadn't really understood that I had been ill for so many years but he turned to someone who was praying with him and said, "This sounds like a bit of attack I think". So he just rebuked these powers of darkness and I went back and sat on my chair. All I could say is that I felt tremendous peace. I didn't know anything had happened. I walked down the aisle to leave the church. Ever since my conversion I had been hearing the voice of the Lord and as I reached the end of the aisle the Lord spoke to me and said, "Today I have healed you of alcoholism, mental illness and of everything. And the outward sign will be that you will never smoke another cigarette again." And I thought, 'Dear Lord, if I give up for two hours it will be a miracle'.

I went home and I realised that I didn't want a cigarette. The Lord told me to buy a bottle of wine for dinner and said he wanted me to have two glasses of that wine. For an alcoholic that is impossible. I hadn't drunk for several years apart from the odd blinder. But the Lord gave me these specific instructions. A girlfriend of mine was coming for supper and both she and David smoked throughout and they just sat there all night staring at me. They couldn't believe it that I didn't smoke and that I appeared to be well. I drank the two glasses of wine and that was it. Normally you can't do that. We would have finished two or three bottles. I used to spend a fiver a day on my cigarettes and the next morning David handed me this fiver and I said, "I don't need it". And he said, "What?" And I said, "I don't need it!" I have never smoked since. There were no withdrawal symptoms, no nothing. But you see the Holy

Spirit spoke to me and said that was to be the outward sign of the miracle he had done in my whole life.

I had just fallen in love with Jesus. I just had this passionate love affair with him. I could then suddenly see why all these saints were in love with Jesus. I was filled with this joy that just so superseded depression that it was unbelievable. Everything became transformed. This dark cottage in Earl's Court just became the joy of my life. We began to open it up to Bible study. I had been under heavy psychiatry and I've still got a letter from the hospital on tiny National Health paper with a note from the psychiatrist saying "Dear Deirdre, I write to confirm that your faith has healed you."

I felt in my bones that in order to stay healed and well I would have to seek God with all my heart. I have tried to do that and the last 14 years have been more exciting and challenging than all the champagne I drank and the jobs I had in the media world.

Deirdre and David Hurst remain prominent congregation members of Holy Trinity Brompton, where they have led home groups for the last 15 years. Deirdre receives invitations to speak about the Christian faith from churches all over the country. She pioneered the daytime Alpha course at HTB – a model which has been taken up by hundreds of other groups.

— oOo —

> "I remember saying to Mum,
> 'If there was a God don't you think he would have
> answered your prayers by now?'"

The story of Mary Stephenson

> *Mary Stephenson's mother prayed all her life that
> her daughter might come to faith in Jesus Christ.
> She watched as Mary became a drug addict, a thief
> and eventually an inmate at Holloway Prison – but
> she never stopped praying. She died in 1987. Here
> Mary describes how her mother's prayers were
> finally answered.*

When I was six weeks old, I was adopted from the
Catholic Children's Adoption Society into a good
home. My adopted father was a diplomat and my mother
was American. My mother was a devout Catholic and
one of the things I truly believe is that it is through her
prayers that I'm here today. I know that she prayed for
me daily. I was raised in South America and when I was
about ten I was sent to a convent boarding school in
England. It was probably then that I started to get quite
independent. It's not like being at day school where you
can go home to Mum and tell her that you're upset about
something. At boarding school I tended to sort out my
problems myself. Sometimes I wouldn't see Mum and
Dad for about four months.

I did my 'A' levels when I was seventeen. One of
them was in theology, but I didn't read the New
Testament so I failed it. There seem to have been so
many times when God has been in my life but I've

ignored him completely because I had no understanding. Nobody explained God to me.

I was off like a shot when I finished school. I moved up to London straight away and got involved with what I thought was a great crowd. I went to all the parties and took something called 'smack' which somebody gave to me saying, "Snort this. It's really fab". So I snorted it up my nose and thought it was such a wonderful feeling. I remember telling a girlfriend of mine, "You've got to try this. It's so good" and she said, "Mary! Smack is heroin". I said, "Don't be so daft." Of course if somebody had handed me a syringe with a needle on the end and said, "Try this", I would have said, "On your bike" because I always thought that heroin, syringes, junkies and Piccadilly Circus went together. But I snorted this apparently quite harmless powder and it was such a nice feeling. I didn't understand what all the fuss was about.

However, it all soon led to 'chasing the dragon' and then mainlining. I spent the next six or seven years leading a life of deceit, dishonesty, lying and whoring...complete abuse. My friends were doing it and I wanted to be involved. To start off with, I used to buy the stuff from them, but as time went on I got to meet the dealers. I really did dive in, but I thought I was all right because I always had a job of some description. I was doing secretarial work at the time. I used to say: "Well, all my other friends who are junkies are unemployed so I can't be that bad because I'm in work." I still had to have a fix to get up in the morning and one at lunch time and one in the evening. But I went to work and I didn't actually realise what sort of state I was in.

I think my brother, who was a medical student at the time, began to notice but I convinced myself that I was leading a normal life. Mum and Dad were abroad, so they didn't really know too much about it. I didn't go home because I never had any money. Occasionally they paid for me to come home and then I used to get quite sick because I was withdrawing. I remember my mother thinking I had rheumatic fever because I was aching and shivering all over. Every time that happened I used to tell myself that I was never going to touch the stuff again. Then, as soon as I got off the plane when I got back to London, I 'scored' straight away.

I became very dishonest and was stealing cheques and things. Inevitably I got caught and at my first court case my Dad really put his career on the line because he stood up in court for me. Unfortunately, the press got hold of it because, although I was nobody, my father was an ambassador in a country at the time. It really broke my parents' heart and, although it wasn't their fault at all, they blamed themselves. I used to say, "I'll be all right, Mum. I'll get my act together now." Then as soon as they went off I'd go back to using.

I ended up in Holloway Prison because I got arrested for stealing. Dealers would acquire stolen cheque books and cheque cards and then they would say, "You go out and buy this" if it was a woman's cheque book and card. So I would pretend to be that person and buy whatever items the dealers wanted – or, more often than not, go into banks and cash the cheque, and get the cash for them – and they would give me drugs in exchange.

What goes on in prison is frightening. I have never been so terrified in my entire life. I couldn't believe what was happening. It's a very frightening and vicious circle and I am very glad that I was only in there for a short spell: about six weeks.

I got out on the condition that I went to a clinic for a year on probation. My parents took me up there and

Mum said to the director, "Where's the nearest Catholic priest or church because I want to contact them so that they know Mary's here?" The director said to Mum, "Look, lady, she's here to get off heroin. Religion? Forget it." I remember saying to Mum, "When are you going to learn? If there was a God, don't you think he would have answered your prayers by now?" She prayed constantly for me.

My parents went back to Canada, where they were living at the time, and I spent a year in this clinic. That was in 1984. At the clinic we were completely humiliated. You began to realise the despair and anguish that you caused other people, but they had a very strange way of doing things. One time I tried to leave and as a result I was dressed in blue overalls and nobody in the clinic spoke to me. There were about 60 people there. My place at the meal table was set upside down and I had to do things like clean the swimming pool with a tea cup and tooth brush. I couldn't understand how they thought that was going to get you off drugs: it seemed it was just to humiliate you.

Unfortunately it all took its toll on my Mum. She had had cancer years before. With all the stress and trauma, it came back in a big way and I know my family felt that I wasn't making things any easier. As soon as I came out of the clinic I 'scored' again with heroin. It was because my mind was not healed: I had been in that clinic through force, and until you yourself decide that you want to do something it just doesn't work. Eventually, though, I did get myself back on my feet and I got good jobs and travelled quite a lot. I got the most fantastic job working in Vancouver. My Mum was dying and it meant that I could go and live there with them as my father was then working in Canada. I had got the job off my own bat as well. I was beginning to feel quite good about myself.

I was with my mother when she died in 1987. She was really at peace when she went. She had an incredible faith. When she died one of the things she said to me was that I would never be happy without faith. She begged me to go to church, the Catholic church, but I thought she was off her rocker. I went on to get good jobs but something was still not quite right. Although I had what I thought were great relationships with men, there was something missing. My oldest friend Daphne had 'got religion' about three or four years before that and she was always telling me to come to church and I would say, "Daphne...Forget it!" I could see that it had made a really, really huge difference to Daphne, which was great, but I said, "It is not for me".

Some time later, I phoned Daphne at nine o'clock one morning before I went to work. I had been out the night before with a load of people and had got absolutely drunk. It was awful because I suddenly found the old feeling of oblivion coming back. I realised that I wasn't happy and I phoned up in tears and Daphne came straight round. She said, "Come on, Mary. Let's pray." So we did and I was in tears, and at that stage I would have gone for anything. She then said, "Why don't you do this Alpha course?"

I went along to the church she suggested and hated it. So I told Daphne where she could put her Alpha course and she said, bless her, "Well look, Mary, I'm going to be helping on a course at another church in April or May. Why don't you do it and then I'll be ᴜnere." So I said: "Well..." And she said: "Oh please, please give it a try." That was the Alpha course at Holy Trinity in April 1993.

I went and when everybody started singing I got very emotional. I found a real warmth and sincerity amongst the people that I hadn't seen before. They really cared. As I listened to the talks, it all began really to fall in place. Mark and Tamsin Carter, my group leaders, are now two of my closest friends. In the first group, Mark said, "What would you like to pray for? Let's all pray for something and we'll see what happens during the course." I was quite selfish and I thought, 'Well all right. I need some real black and white signs here'. I said I wanted to pray for more gallery sales (I was working in a sculpture gallery) because things were absolutely dead. He said, "All right, that's fine. Anything else?" And I said – I was being a bit flippant – "Pray that I come back next week maybe."

The following week I sold £85,000 worth of sculpture which I thought was a coincidence, but I went back because I felt that I had to go back and tell them.

I went back each week to Alpha, and soon it was time for the weekend away on the subject of the Holy Spirit. I didn't know whether I actually wanted to spend the weekend with a bunch of Christians. As it turned out, it was a very, very powerful weekend for me. Minutes into the first talk I was in floods of tears, and started shaking and sobbing. It was a very powerful feeling, but it was really safe. I can't compare to it anything I'd ever experienced before. I am so used to myself being dishonest that I would expect other people to be the same but it was wonderful and there was no doubt that God started working in my life.

On the Sunday morning James Odgers, who was leading the weekend, asked the Holy Spirit to come and said, "All those of you who want to ask Jesus Christ into your lives can say this prayer" and he said a short prayer. I said it and I *really* said it. I asked God into my life and I asked him to sort me out. That really did happen. He came in to my life but I still felt unworthy. It wasn't until a Sunday service later on that I actually felt that I had been forgiven. People saw me in tears and it didn't matter because I knew I was safe to do it in front of those people. I am completely cleansed and God has given me the most fantastic sign of his love.

I recently moved to a flat in North Kensington and soon afterwards I was on my way home when I saw a woman who had dropped her shopping. I helped her pick it up and as I looked up I saw a sign which said 'Catholic Children's Adoption Society'. It is right at the end of my road. I called my father and said, "Dad, did you get me from the Catholic Children's Adoption Society in St Charles Square?" He said, "Yes that's right." After that, I went round and round on my moped looking at it and I thought, 'God really has wiped my slate clean. He's brought me back to start my life again from where I started it.' I felt God saying, "Thirty-something years ago you started your life here. You went off down the wrong road and now I'm giving it back to you." He has given it back to me and I've given my life back to him now. It's so true when the Bible says how God restores the years the locusts have eaten.

There were some people I hurt where I might never be able to make amends: one of those is my Mum...I'm sure she's doing somersaults up there now. For once I am so content. I had never cried before, but at church I have cried a lot. The point is that there's always somebody there. Even if I'm at home alone and I'm crying, I know I'm not alone any more because God is there. That is a real comfort. I remember thinking the other night how I always used to have my fix next to my bedside table and

I'd have a fix before I went to bed at night and then get it ready to have first thing in the morning. Now I've replaced that with my Bible. And I'm more passionate about the Bible than I ever was about my heroin. Indeed, my passion for heroin has been replaced by a far greater passion for Jesus Christ.

Mary Stephenson now works part-time for St Stephen's Church, Westbourne Park – a 'plant' from Holy Trinity Brompton – where she is secretary of the church council. She is also chairman of Peake House, a Christian hostel for ex-offenders, and the Blenheim Project, which runs a drop-in centre for drug addicts. She says, "Basically my life has completely changed."

> "... God has decided on an even better plan for us"
> *Hebrews 11:40*

2

"I thought that if God was alive then he must be extraordinarily boring and certainly not worth getting to know."

The story of Charlie Mackesy

> *Artist Charlie Mackesy has had some 25 exhibitions of his work in galleries in Britain and America. Here he tells the story of how he became a Christian and the effect it had on his life:*

I was a chapel-hater at school. We had chapel every night and I was the principal belcher and disrupter of services. I enjoyed disturbing them because they were so tedious. I loathed the smell – the stink of polish – and I hated the way men wore dresses. I thought that if God was alive then he must be extraordinarily boring and certainly not worth getting to know. Christians around me didn't seem to have anything that I desired at all. They seemed to be the small-minded and bickering type.

I went through both state and private education. I was

a very restless and rebellious student. I felt that there must be more to life than the wife/career/house/mortgage/pension/death plan that was on offer. After leaving school, I ended up as a shepherd in Gloucestershire. I worked during the day and then drank for England every night with the same group of friends in the same pub. I left the farm and went on an extended binge, ending up staying with my sister in London. She was great. I guess she had to be. While there, I remember being on the tube one day when an old lady collapsed and businessmen, who I had been brought up to believe were 'refined and virtuous', climbed over her to get to work. I began to think that if man was the pinnacle of things, then it was a very sad situation – although there were some glorious attributes to him.

I was going out to parties and smoking a lot of drugs and drinking. I did it because everybody else did it and it was fine. I think I was a bit of a pioneer on the lunatic fringe. I started streaking at public events and getting into the tabloids. I was pictured naked in the *Daily Mirror* once – half a page. Fortunately it was a rear view so I was unrecognisable – but my landlady dropped the paper next to my cornflakes muttering, "Honestly, the things they get up to these days". It wasn't that I wanted to display my body. It's just that I was so bored by everything. Once I streaked at Badminton horse trials and I swam through the water jump. It appeared on TV when my Dad was watching. I'm glad he didn't recognise me – Christmas would have been a nightmare. We were chased by the police, but I was hidden by the crowd. People surrounded me and kept giving me clothes, saying, "Put this on. Put this on."

I continued drinking and partying, but ironically this was a thinking time for me. One time I was fixing a puncture on my bicycle just outside the house. It was a very hot day and I said in my heart – I'm not really sure why – "Jesus Christ, I don't know who you are. To me you've been a fluffy person in a manger or an aryan blue-eyed floating person wandering around saying, 'Bless you my child'. I'll wipe away my arrogant preconceptions and ask you who you are." I didn't hear any voice. I didn't experience any bright lights or conversion things – but two nights later I was at a party where I used to take drugs. I was dancing wildly and really enjoying myself and someone came up to me and asked me what drug I was on. I looked at him and realised I had not taken anything and yet I felt very free. This was quite disturbing. I could not understand it. Could my prayers have something to do with it?

Within a month my best friend was killed in a car accident. At the funeral I was screaming in my heart because he was the closest friend I ever had. I was saying "Why?" There was no real reply at all. The irony was that it made me more aware of God rather than less, even though I didn't understand why it happened. I just had to acknowledge him. I didn't know how to pray so I used to write down my prayers – often on the side of drawings. I was aware of a constant loving surveillance by this God who I didn't really know.

I did not go to church, because I couldn't make the connection between this love I had experienced and the dreary place that church was to me then. I sometimes used to wander into empty chapels and sit at the back. One Sunday morning while spending a weekend in Cirencester partying with friends, I was woken up by the sound of church bells in the morning and went along. I felt almost drawn to it. There were five old ladies in furry hats at the front with the vicar. Usual stuff. I remember saying to God, "Is this really your place?" I grabbed a book, which turned out to be a Bible. I had never enjoyed reading it. I just happened to open it to the Gospel of John and read and re-read John 10:10, which says, "I have come to give you life that you may have it to the full." I just stared at it in disbelief because it made total sense. I wanted to pick up the old ladies at the front and hug them and bounce them up and down. I managed to resist. I saw that the person who had been inside me since I said that prayer with the bike was the same person who said these things. I started going to a little church in Fulham and I was the youngest by 45 years. I became their sort of "mascot" and I enjoyed that.

My gift of painting was very much related to my experiences of Jesus Christ. On the day that I was fixing my bicycle and said that prayer, I picked up a Rotring pen and started drawing. Before then, I had hardly done any drawing at all. The two things were simultaneous.

I still didn't think any Christians existed under the age of 65 but I was happy with that. I was quite happy with God and just enjoying him alone. I was living with a girlfriend in a flat in Earl's Court at the time. I met a guy at a dinner party and I told him I was a Christian. He obviously did not believe me and consequently took me off to hear a guy called Luis Palau speak. I listened to him and when he asked people to come forward I thought, 'This is it'. I was quite scared really. There was a Christian counsellor there and I asked if it was wrong to be living with a girlfriend. His eyes bulged and he nearly choked. I was aware deep down that something was wrong with our relationship. I had this gentle sense of pain in my heart and felt that something wasn't right about the way we were living. I told my girlfriend and she thought I had gone insane. Pretty soon I had moved into another flat and she was living elsewhere. (She is now married and a Christian.)

Having got drunk regularly with the lads, I gradually found I was spending less time on the floor. It seemed I had more life without it. A couple of years later, I ended up quite by chance at Holy Trinity Brompton. I had started doing drawings for estate agents and had been commissioned by Knight, Frank and Rutley to do a painting of a small section of the Brompton Oratory. I went to HTB to sit down because it was quiet and away from the road. I walked into the church and sat there in a pew with no reason to believe that it was anything different from any of the other churches I had seen. But for some reason I decided to go one Sunday night. I can't remember why. But I walked in and there were 800 people of my age jumping up and down singing. Traumas. I skulked behind the pillars for five Sundays and didn't meet anyone. I just stared. Then Nicky Gumbel [*HTB curate*] came up to me and invited me to a pastorate group. I cringed because it was people sipping coffee and talking about religion. It totally horrified me. But I persevered with it and some of the people who were in that group are now my closest friends. Nicky Gumbel was the first Christian I really respected, loved and listened to. I absolutely adored him. We often used to sit and chortle about everything under the sun.

My understanding of scripture came through his pastorate. Beforehand my faith had been purely subjective. I had no concept of theology. I did not understand the cross. I did not understand what Jesus Christ had done. I just enjoyed him.

When I was painting I became very aware of the Holy Spirit in the room. I used to do embarrassing things like clap and giggle. It felt like he was encouraging me to paint things that expressed what I felt about him. At this time, Jesus became a laugh – a good friend. But now, after discovering what he has done, it is far more serious than I ever realised. He's moved from being just a friend to being Lord. That's quite a transition because he wasn't Lord before. Now I have this horrific awe of him. The joy and the friendship hasn't changed but I think my understanding of who he is has changed. I'm no angel – I'm still a pig-headed, argumentative person – but he's dealing with that.

I do a lot of speaking in schools. Chapels and stuff. I had to prepare something recently and was reading that the wicked should 'drink from the cup of the wrath of the Almighty' and I realised that was the cup Jesus was talking about when he said "if it's possible, let it be taken from me". It's the wrath I should have taken that he took. Outrageous. I have come to see that Christianity is about living life to the full with God – with passion. I've learned that it's all right to sing my head off to God – and that it's not insane. I can't describe what I feel for Jesus, but my love for him is completely consuming. As a person, I am restless, fickle and get bored easily. There are only two things I have stuck at in my life – Jesus and my painting.

With Jesus I know there is nowhere else to go. He is my hope, my focus, my horizon. He is wild.

Charlie Mackesy remains a member of Holy Trinity Brompton. He speaks about Christianity at school assemblies all over the country. His paintings continue to be in great demand.

— oOo —

"My perception of church was all blue rinses and hats and little old ladies in the front row....
What had it got to offer me? Nothing."

The story of Richard Ward

Fitness executive Richard Ward was rollerblading in Hyde Park one Sunday afternoon when he met a girl who, after a brief chat, said she was off to church. He decided to go along with her. That was the start of a series of events which have changed his life. Here he tells the story of what happened:

From as early as I can remember we never went to church as a family. It wasn't something that anybody in my family ever did. I went to a Quaker boarding school – but only because it was the school my father went to. There was very little religious education there. It was either RE or history and I chose history. We had 'meetings' in the mornings and on Sundays – but they were often just times of silence. If someone talked, it was not necessarily about the Bible. I was asleep or reading a book in the back row. It didn't interest me at all.

As soon as I left school I went to live in the States. I was a sky-diving instructor and I used to jump out of planes for a living. I did every dangerous sport that there was, including scuba diving, sky diving, and base-jumping (jumping off buildings, antennas, bridges, and cliffs with a parachute). I was doing all of that for about five years or so – and was also enjoying women, drinking every day, and partying all night. I was leading a very wild lifestyle.

Then I came back to England. My father was dying. While in the States I had done some courses in fitness and I came back here and continued my education in physical education and psychology. I managed to get work in a gym doing instructing, aerobics and that sort of stuff. I worked my way up from instructor to assistant manager to manager to running a very successful club in Berkshire with 4,500 members. It was one of the top clubs in the country.

I went after status and money and that sort of thing and progressed from that club into customer services in the fitness industry. I became Customer Service Director of a company which put all the equipment – like the treadmills and the bikes – into the gyms. It was a very good job, with good money, a car and so on. While I was doing that I took up rollerblading and, as was my way, I spent some time chasing pretty women.

One Sunday afternoon in June last year, I was chasing

this pretty woman in Hyde Park on rollerblades. We started chatting when suddenly she said, "I'm out of here. I've got to go." So I said, "Where are you going?" and she said, "To church. Do you want to come?" So I said, "Yeah, OK."

It was just another avenue to stay with her for the rest of the evening. My perception of church was all blue rinses and hats and little old ladies in the front row. It was something that I did not want to be a part of. What had it got to offer me? Nothing. So we came in and sat near the back. It was a normal service for HTB – not that I knew what a normal service was – and I found it rather boring. Everybody else sang and I didn't. I was struck that many of the people there were my age and younger, but I just kind of stood there because I thought it was the thing to do.

I'd been to weddings and funerals. I never used to sing or pray or anything. I just used to stand there. Then, at the end of the service, the ministry started and these strange things were happening. I thought, 'What is this?' People were falling over and being filled with the Spirit and I thought, 'What is going on here?' I've always had a very inquisitive nature and it kind of sparked an interest to understand why all these people were doing this. So I kept on coming back – not for the girl, but for my own intellect and wanting to know more about what was going on. I came back for the whole of that summer – every Sunday. I wasn't even living in London at the time. I was living out near Bracknell. It was a long way to come but I always made the excuse that I was coming rollerblading on a Sunday. I used to come rollerblading in Hyde Park and come in to church in the evening.

I can remember someone mentioning Alpha in one service. It was starting in October and I talked to some people about it and they said, "O yeah, you should really do this." I was going away on business for the whole of November so there wasn't much point in starting something that I wasn't going to finish, so I didn't do it. I came back to find there was another Alpha course starting in January and I decided to come along to that one.

I still wasn't a Christian and was very apprehensive when I walked in. I was expecting maybe 30 or 40 people and there were 600 people all milling around in the church. I was put into a group and what struck me was that the people were so normal. There was a real cross-section of the community. But when I looked at the group, I thought, 'I'm afraid I have nothing in common with any of these people'. After a week, I thought I'd keep coming back, even though I was driving up to London from Bracknell. As the weeks went on, the group got on exceptionally well together. I found things that we did have in common. I also found the talks interesting. I've come from a background where unless you can prove something to me, I'm not going to believe it. I was seeing some things in those first five weeks or so, but nothing really clicked.

Then we went away on the Alpha weekend and I drove up to London to pick up Neville, my group leader, and a couple of others. We were going to Pontins at Chichester. I hadn't told anybody what I was doing on Wednesdays and only told a few people that I was going away for the weekend. I certainly told nobody that I was going to Pontins! No-one! Normally I'm the kind of person who talks quite a lot – I'm quite outgoing – but on the Friday night driving down, Neville and the others were surprised how quiet I was. I was actually driving along and thinking, 'I don't really want to be here.' In fact I wouldn't have gone on the weekend at all if I hadn't had to come up to London to pick them up. Half way down to Chichester, I thought that I'd just drop them off and leave them. I'd just be their taxi getting down. When we got there, I went to the bar and had a couple of drinks and, seeing all the normal people there, I ended up staying.

On the Saturday we had a couple of talks and that afternoon we discussed spiritual gifts in our small group. I just sat there and said, "I just don't get this. I don't understand at all." They just said, "Don't worry, don't worry..." I was getting really wound up by this point. I just wanted to leave. But I guess I kept on thinking that there was something in all that I was hearing. I just didn't want to give in.

That evening, Nicky spoke and at the end he said, "If anyone wants to pray this prayer giving their lives to Jesus Christ, here it is..." By that time I thought, 'OK, I've got nothing else to lose. Let me do it.' And I did and I meant it. I said sorry for the things I had done in the past, asked Jesus into my life, and turned away from everything I knew that was bad. I really prayed it in my heart. At that point I just felt this total forgiveness and peace. I fell over and I remember I couldn't move. The people in the group said I fell just after Nicky had invited the Holy Spirit to come and move amongst us. I went over, bang. They had been really worried for me because throughout the day they had thought I definitely wasn't going to enjoy this. They thought I would certainly want to go home. They couldn't believe it.

When I fell over, I just felt a real inner peace that everything that I had done in the past – and I'd done a lot – had been forgiven. I was crying as I lay there. Then it turned to laughter. When I got up, I just had this glow. Prior to that I had rarely smiled. Then suddenly I just had this beaming grin on my face. Just before dinner, Neville said he thought I needed a drink. So we went to buy one and I couldn't drink anything. I just kept on laughing and laughing. It was just hysterical laughter. I couldn't stop. Somebody would say something and I would just burst into hysterical laughter. I've never been an emotional person. I never laughed or cried. But I was crying on the floor and then laughing. Eventually I calmed down and sat down at the dinner table. There was a choice of menu and the others on the table said, "What would you like for a starter Richard? Would you like the French Onion soup?" And I just burst into laughter. I don't know why. It got everybody else going and I thought, 'What is going on here?' Again I calmed down. But every time they mentioned French Onion soup, I'd just crack up with laughter.

All evening, I was on a real high. It was just wonderful. I've never experienced that sort of thing before. I've always suppressed my feelings to everybody and I've never been outward with any of my emotions. I've always kept them inside. I didn't want to show anyone how I was feeling. I came back and the next week was excellent. I had a really good time. Everybody at work said, "Wow, what's happened?"

I was a bit of an ogre at work – a bit of a slave driver. I always put in long hours – working maybe from seven in the morning to nine at night every day – and I expected everybody else to do it. When I got back from the weekend I woke up to what I was doing. I realised I shouldn't expect everybody else to do as much as I did – and I also wondered if I myself should be doing so much. I was taking a lot of pressure on myself at work and was getting very stressed out.

I changed quite considerably in ways that I wasn't

expecting. I didn't pressure people, saying "Why haven't you done this? I asked you to do this yesterday, why isn't it done now?" I mellowed out a bit and didn't expect so much of people. I also had a passion for reading the Bible which I had never had.

I heard that there was another Alpha weekend the following weekend and I asked if I could go. There were three from my course who didn't go the first week and I drove them down. We had a great time. It was also my birthday that weekend as well. Everyone sang 'Happy Birthday' to me and I couldn't believe it. I kept thinking, 'But you don't even know me'.

At around this time I had a major 'downer' and for two days I was on a real low. I phoned around Neville and people in my group asking them to help me out. I began thinking, "What am I doing? My whole past life has been good and I am throwing it away..." The following Wednesday I didn't want to come back, but I did and I drove up and sat in the car park for 20 minutes.

I think the main reason I came back was that I had made such good friends over five weeks with the people in my group. I came back more for them than for myself really. Nicky prayed for me because Neville saw that he really couldn't deal with it – and I guess I came out of it in the end.

The main thing to say is that it's not easy. It wasn't easy and it hasn't been easy. Things have completely turned around in my life. There were some attitudes within the company where I was working which I couldn't condone any more. I simply couldn't do some of the things I was asked to do any more. I was very honest with the company. I told them I was going to have to leave unless certain things changed within this company. They weren't willing to change them, so I handed in my notice and gave up my job.

After giving up my job, I had three offers for other work within the space of a week. I didn't take any of them. I just didn't feel right about taking something right on again. I had worked 18 months solidly without a day off. I just wanted to take some time. Now I pray about everything I do. I do it for Jesus. I'm not now doing it for myself any more. I read the Bible daily – morning and evening. And now that I have spare time I'm reading it all the time.

Something I've never done is help other people out. I used to think, 'I'm looking after myself. I've got no time for you...' I'm looking after other people now and helping them out, praying for them. I know that God has forgiven all my past. I am going to have eternal life with him. I speak about God and Jesus all the time – as much as I can – to people that I possibly don't even know. I've been up to Speakers' Corner with somebody in my Home Group. We went up there and we were talking about Jesus, something I would never do.

I believe everybody should be able to hear this or have the opportunity to make up their own mind. It is almost as if I just suddenly woke up and my eyes were washed clean. Until that very moment I didn't know that what I was doing was wrong. You name it. I was doing it – but I've turned away from it all now. I don't need to do it any more.

Richard Ward continues to be a member of Holy Trinity Brompton, where he helps out on the church's Alpha course.

— oOo —

"When I tried worshipping God, all I could think about was how I wished I was listening to heavy metal."

The story of Richard Daniell

> *On the last night of Focus '93, Holy Trinity Brompton's teaching holiday week, Sandy Millar invited anyone to come up to the stage to say something of what God had done for them during the week. Richard Daniell was first on the stage and told of how he had become a Christian two months before and how his life had changed. He paid tribute to his parents who had always prayed for him. Here he tells the story:*

I grew up as a Christian with very good guidance from my parents. I knew all the Christian basics but as a teenager I rebelled against them. We were living in Germany because my father worked for an American company there. At 13 I got into things like stealing and vandalism – basically because I wanted to impress people. We used to jump over cars – on the bonnet and on the roof. I got caught once when we jumped over a number of cars in a row and did a lot of damage, but no-one pressed charges. I started stealing at the same time. I got caught by the police stealing something in one of the huge supermarkets that they have in Germany. I was concerned about what my parents would think, but I didn't think stealing was wrong. I just continued doing it. I didn't steal anything big – just T-shirts, records, tapes, and things. I didn't do it because I didn't have any money but because I thought it impressed my mates.

When I was 18, I had a very bad relationship with a girlfriend. She was into the occult, on drugs, drink – all sorts – and I thought I could change her. I had planned to marry her and had all these fantastic plans, but she cheated on me and went off with some other chap which really hurt me. That is when I decided that stealing and vandalism were wrong and I adopted nearly all the Christian morals – no sex-before-marriage, no stealing, no vandalism, no drinking – without becoming a Christian.

I went to York University and one of the ways I tried to get over the relationship was that I got into heavy metal music. I remember listening to AC/DC to get over it. I'd put it on really loud and felt reassured by the power. It gave me a sense of power. Then I got into Iron Maiden and Guns 'n' Roses. I used to put it on when I was feeling depressed or lonely and it made me feel better.

Last May I got really desperate because I didn't know what I was going to do after University. I tried for Personnel Management but that fell through. I tried to do a Post Graduate Study but it didn't work out. At the same time lots and lots of problems that had accumulated over my 21 years came to the surface. They were all desperate things that I was concerned about and knew I couldn't solve. That's when I said, "Look I've got to try Christianity out. I've got to trust God and see if he's really there and if he cares for me." So I bought a Bible – the cheapest one I could find in case it didn't work out – and a devotional. All the first verses in the devotional were very basic scripture, saying, "Be courageous, stand up. The Lord will be with you." Others were basic about sin – Jesus Christ dying on the cross for my sin. They were about redemption, atonement, and all the basic principles which I didn't quite understand at the time.

Then I started knowing I had to do stuff. I knew I had to take down my posters. I knew I had to throw away my heavy metal tapes. But the first big step I made concerned something called the 'Dead Pool'. I lived with three other lads and in our living room we had this thing called the 'Dead Pool'. We each had a list of ten people whom we predicted would die in the near future. We had a deal that if one of the people that we'd predicted died, all the others had to give that person £2 for it. The list was kept on the wall in the living room. My Mum came up a few months back and she called it a death wish, which was perfectly right, but we didn't see it that way. We thought it was harmless. But it had been playing on my conscience ever since she said that, but I kept on with it because it was fun.

When I became a Christian, I knew that I'd have to tell my other friends that I wanted my list crossed off. I went into the living room one night, and it was only Alistair there and I knew that God was telling me that it was evil and I had to get off it. But I couldn't tell him. I really wanted to obey so I went upstairs to the bathroom, and I said, "Lord, give me strength. I know I've got to tell him. Lord just be with me!" And I went down again, and with a very nervous tingly voice, I said, "Alistair, it's been bothering my conscience. Do you mind if I get off the 'Dead Pool'?" I added, "You can continue it if you want, but I want to be off it."

This was the first way that God moved greatly. I was so shocked with what Alistair said. He said to me, "Richard, perhaps you're right. Maybe it is wrong." I was so shocked by the answer. I had expected him to mock me. After that, I felt God really filling me, and comforting me. I felt so good. I felt such joy. I'd got through it.

I knew I had to get involved with other Christians and began meeting members of the university Christian Union. After the first small group, I told Alistair and my other friend Mike that I'd become a Christian. I thought they would shut me out and hate me – we'd all been so anti-Christian before, making jokes about how boring Christians were. But they were wonderful. They said it was great.

I went to *Focus '93* with my parents, who had heard about it through family friends. The first night, I got together with one of the pastoral groups and we went to the pub. It was a really good experience. I could see love pouring out of them all. But I was really uneasy about worshipping God, and the main reason for this was the heavy metal music that I'd been listening to. I went to a seminar on worship and I really struggled. When I tried worshipping God, all I could think about was how I wished I was listening to heavy metal. I thought this worshipping stuff was pretty weak. Two of the worship leaders prayed for me and asked the Holy Spirit to fill me and to cleanse me of the heavy metal. One of them, Andy, said that heavy metal was very small, and that Jesus Christ is infinite. I went away still confused, but I prayed, and said, "Lord, heal me. I really want to worship you."

I felt God tell me I just had to be me when I worshipped – to stop trying to be someone else. I should worship how I wanted to worship. That evening I started enjoying worshipping, and session after session I enjoyed worshipping more and more. At a session of teaching about the 'Father's blessing', I felt the power of the Holy Spirit for the first time. I went up to be blessed by God. After that I knew God loved me, cared for me and had a great plan for me.

Then my Dad came up and gave me his own 'blessing', and after that I felt great. There had been a few uneasy tensions between my Dad and me. I thought we couldn't relate, but that's been healed. I spent most of the last day reading my Bible. I went on the beach for an hour and wrote down all the things God had taught me and thanked him for it. I felt really restored. By the evening I was really ready for the celebration. I worshipped as I'd never worshipped before!

My parents have always prayed for me. I am so grateful.

After Focus '93, Richard Daniell spent one and a half years as a volunteer youth leader for a Christian organisation called 'Young Life' in Dusseldorf. He then spent six months on a Discipleship Training School with missionary organisation Youth with a Mission in Switzerland. He is now about to start a teacher training course in London. He says, "Since Focus '93, God has continued to be so faithful in my life. He has guided me every step of the way."

"... you restored my life."
Psalm 30:3

3

"It seemed to me that a finger was pointing down on to a TV screen and God was saying, 'Watch this space, because what's about to happen, I am going to make happen.'"

The story of James and Anna Wynn

James and Anna Wynn had been separated for two years when James became a Christian in 1987. Here, in a transcript of a conversation 48 hours after the birth of his first daughter, he tells the extraordinary story of how God brought them back together when their divorce was just days from completion.

Anna and I got married in 1983. She was ten years younger than me and had only just left university. The breakdown in our marriage came about slowly. We had our own careers and I was pursuing mine very aggressively.

I was working for the BBC, which is not exactly an easy place, and Anna was working hard trying to establish a career in publishing. We communicated less and less on any meaningful level and failed to recognise each other's needs. Basically we were on two parallel tracks. We parted and although we tried to get back together lots of times, the split became wider and wider.

When we broke up I began earnestly searching for some meaning to life. I didn't think to look to the church because that was boring, so I looked at things that seemed more of the moment. For me that was the New Age movement.

In 1987, two years after Anna and I had broken up, I was working with Sarah Jarman [*a member of Holy Trinity Brompton*] at the BBC on the Noel Edmonds Christmas Show and we were going by train to do a recce in Cornwall. I told her a little about my situation, which she knew because we were in the same office. I mentioned this New Age thing and she said, "Why don't you come to church?"

I thought, 'Well, OK.' I remember a pause in our conversation when I knew she was praying. She didn't pray out loud but she just closed her eyes and looked out of the window. I didn't mind, but I thought it was odd.

A couple of weeks later I showed up at HTB. I didn't really know what was going on but I could see it was something quite powerful. I started going on my own. Suddenly I found Bible verses began coming into my mind, although I hadn't read the Bible for ages.

Then one particular night I drove home and there was a card from Anna. It was December 14th, 1987. It said, "I was thinking about you the other day with Christmas coming up" – and a few other things. I remember reading it and the pain of the whole thing swamped me.

I was in the kitchen and I knelt down and prayed, with tears absolutely flooding down my face. I said, "God if you're there, please show me." I think that's all I said but I prayed it like I'd never prayed anything.

Then I went to the phone and picked up the card from HTB and saw Nicky's name [*Nicky Gumbel, HTB curate*] on the back. I knew that he was the guy who had spoken when I first went. I couldn't remember what he'd said but I knew that he was funny and that I could relate to him. I phoned him up and said, "Look, you don't know me, but I heard you speaking and I think I'd like to come and talk to you because something's going on and I don't understand it." He suggested we met the next day. I went to bed and woke up in the middle of the night having had what I can only describe as an extraordinary vision.

I went to work the next day and then went to see Nicky at lunch time. We went across the road to a rather smart wine bar. We got talking and he pulled out a Bible which I thought was really weird! It was mid-week and he had a Bible in a wine bar! Anyway, we came back to the church and he talked a little bit and asked me what I thought was happening. I said, "Well, I think God's speaking to me." He agreed. So we went to the Crypt, where I prayed a prayer of Christian commitment. He said it was like a bench mark, and that I'd probably prayed it already but hadn't formalised it. I asked Jesus to forgive me and to come in and take over my life. I didn't feel anything. It was no big deal and I went back to work.

Thereafter, Nicky was brilliant. He would call me to ask me how I was. He said he knew that God could do the impossible but he didn't say that he would bring

Anna back. I was praying the whole time that she would come back. I don't think there was a day that I didn't. Sometimes I thought things were going to happen and other times I didn't think anything was going to happen. But I still prayed. I told Anna I'd become a Christian. We weren't seeing each other at all, but she did agree to go and see Nicky and Pippa [*Nicky's wife*].

In the meantime, the divorce was going through. The real crunch came when the divorce papers arrived and I had to make a decision about whether or not to sign them. I took myself away one weekend and felt God saying, "Sign them and trust me." It was the very last thing I wanted to do, but I had so many indications along the way that it was right. I signed and put the letter in the post thinking, 'Well that's it now, but I'll still go on praying.'

In the meantime, Anna had moved out of London and gone to Oxford and bought a house with her then boyfriend. The signs were pretty grim to be honest. Then a remarkable thing happened. Billy Graham was doing a mission in London and as I had just finished a long stint at Granada TV in Manchester, I was able to give some time to help. I drove people and literature around London for a couple of weeks. During that time, I met an old couple in the back of a taxi. In about two minutes I gave them my story. They said, "OK James, we'll pray for you and your wife." I said, "Great." I left them at their hotel and drove off.

About three days later, I 'happened' to bump into them in the street. They said, "Hi, the Lord gave us a picture for you, James – for you and your wife. We think it's for you." I thought, 'Oh no'. Then they said, "The Lord gave us this verse for you." It was from Numbers 11:23, "The Lord answered Moses, 'Is my arm too short? You will now see whether or not what I say will come true for you.'" We had about two weeks to go before the decree nisi and it seemed to me that a finger was pointing down on to a TV screen and God was saying, "Watch this space, because what's about to happen, I am going to make happen, and I want you to know that now so that when it does, you'll know it's me."

By this stage I'd sent Anna some tickets to Billy Graham and she'd said, "Sorry, can't come." I sent her two more tickets because Billy Graham had decided to stay for another week. I went on praying. On Wednesday the decree nisi arrived, and on Thursday Anna called me up and said she'd got the other tickets and would like to go with me. I hadn't been asking her to go with me so needless to say I was quite surprised! We went the following Saturday.

We hadn't seen each other for two and a half years but as we drove to Wembley I felt remarkably peaceful. There seemed no way we were going to get back together. We sat down without saying much. Billy Graham spoke and the next thing I knew was that when he invited people who wanted to commit their lives to Jesus to go forward, Anna ran forward. I was just crying and crying. I was so overcome.

The next morning we went to church at St Paul's Onslow Square. Nicky came up and was asking all these questions like, "Did it rain?" and "Was it wet on the pitch?" He didn't want to ask straight out if Anna had gone forward. He couldn't look at us while he was preaching. It was brilliant for Anna because Nicky spoke on the Cross and it explained all that had happened the day before.

Anna went back to Oxford. She prayed a lot and had some amazing answers but it wasn't easy, especially for her boyfriend. She came down to the Alpha course each week and Pippa bought her a Bible. Pippa telephoned Anna regularly and found her somewhere else to live in Oxford because she had to continue her job. We knew straight after Anna's conversion that we were going to be back together.

Before the decree absolute came through, we went to court and told them we wanted our divorce files thrown away. The judge was delighted. He said, "I sit here day after day hearing these terrible stories. It's so wonderful to hear this!" As we were leaving, the usher ran out after us and said:"We never have any good news around here."

We had a blessing service at Holy Trinity Brompton to re-dedicate our marriage vows to God. He had saved our marriage at the very last hour but we still had a lot to work through together which wasn't always easy.

We also wanted children. God was blessing us in every area, but our most cherished desire wasn't happening. It was the toughest thing. For three years we were constantly living between hope and disappointment. All around us people were having children.

Many, many people prayed for us but we finally got to the stage of agreeing to a course of treatment. We continued to pray that it would happen naturally.

We went on holiday knowing that we were coming back to start treatment on the Monday. On Thursday morning, Anna was feeling sick. I thought it might be serious. She was very weak and couldn't ski.

We'd been through so many pregnancy tests in the past that I think we had been keeping the industry afloat. It seemed the last possibility that Anna could be pregnant. That morning I went down to a Swiss chemist and in my best French tried to say I wanted a pregnancy test kit.

Anna did the test and announced, "I'm pregnant." We didn't believe it, so I went back to get another one. We did it again and the same thing happened.

Then Anna said she wanted a sign from God, so we looked at the Bible. We just let it fall open – all the things you're not supposed to do – and it opened at a verse in Isaiah, which was, "'In the time of my favour, I will answer you,' says the Lord." We came back and told the hospital that we didn't need the treatment any more.

Abigail weighed 6 pounds 11 ounces. 'Abigail' means 'Father rejoiced' and we like the name for that reason. She's wonderful! I sometimes wonder why God has done things this way in my life and the truth is I don't really know. All I do know is that I can't look at Anna or Abigail without thinking of him.

James and Anna Wynn are members of the congregation at Holy Trinity Brompton. Their second daughter, Julia Charlotte, was born on July 4th, 1995.

— oOo —

"I said, 'Look, I nearly died of cancer when I was 30. I find life pretty difficult and not a great deal of fun and ... eternal life is the last thing I want.'"

The story of Robert Taylor

Robert Taylor had left his wife and children and was living alone in a flat when he was first told about Holy Trinity Brompton's Alpha course. He went on the course in October 1994. Today he is back with his family. Here he tells the moving story of what happened to him:

I was baptised as a child, but I didn't go to church at all. My family didn't go. The only times I went were for my wedding, my brother's wedding and a couple of funerals. When I was 30 – eleven years ago – I had cancer. I had major surgery, followed by six months' chemotherapy and three months' radiotherapy. At one stage it didn't look like it was going to work. I was down to under nine stone and bald as a coot. But the last two treatments did the trick. Although I thought I might die, I didn't turn to God at all.

Then, in May 1994, a friend I had met when training to be a chartered accountant asked me out for a drink and suggested that I go on an Alpha course at Holy Trinity Brompton. He knew that my marriage was going through considerable difficulty and he wanted to help. He thought that my going on an Alpha Course would be a step in the right direction. I had been married for 16 years and had two children, one aged six and the other aged four. I had decided that my marriage was not recoverable and had left home the previous February. I told him that I would think about doing Alpha, but I had no intention of going. I just thought he was one of these very nice well-meaning Christian chaps but it really wasn't for me.

So I just carried on living the life of a single person in London. I had quite a senior job as a company treasurer at the time. I was hectic in business and hectic socially as well. Then, four months later, I went out for lunch with a banking colleague of mine and at the end of the lunch, during which we had had quite a lot of very nice claret, he suggested I went on the Alpha Course at HTB. I felt that that was rather a coincidence.

The friend who had asked me to go on the course four months before had given me a copy of *Questions of Life* and *Why Jesus?*, by Nicky Gumbel, so I started reading them – and then I thought I might go on the course. Wednesday nights were usually a quieter night for me and I thought I might meet some interesting people. I had no intention of becoming a Christian. I still didn't go for the first two sessions, but then my banking friend, Nick Saint, sent me an NIV Bible and tapes of the first two Alpha talks. In a very relaxed way, not putting me under pressure, he said, "Look, you should listen to these and really you should come along."

So I went to the third session and I was really very nervous. I didn't sing a single song. I was very tense and agitated. Then I went into the small groups. Bruce Streather [*a member of the HTB congregation*] was leading my group and I decided to make it quite clear that I wasn't interested in any of this. I said, "Look, I nearly died of cancer when I was 30. I find life pretty difficult and not a great deal of fun and as far as I am concerned, eternal life is the last thing I want. So I really can't see what Christianity's got to offer me."

That cast a bit of a pall over the group. They all went a bit quiet. Then Bruce said, "Well that's a very interesting point of view." After that, I just listened to the group's discussion. Everybody seemed to be having quite a good time and there were one or two people in the group I could relate to, so I thought 'Well, I'll come back next week'.

After that, I started to listen to the talks. I remember Nicky telling the story about the time he went to referee a football match when he knew absolutely nothing about football and all the children started kicking each other and getting hurt. He explained that it was very important to have a set of rules, and if you have a set of rules, then people enjoy themselves a lot better and nobody gets hurt. I related to that. I really had no point of reference about how I should conduct my life. I had just conducted it how I wanted to live it. Because I had nearly died when I was 30, I was extremely selfish saying, "Well look, I want to get as much out of this life as I can. I'm only here once." So gradually I started to realise that Christianity could give me that reference point and that perhaps my life would be better if I stuck to some rules. Then, once I had decided that there was something in the rules, I started to listen quite a bit more intently and I think I started to say, "Well look, if this is true, then I can't really ignore it."

So it became a big issue of whether it was true or not. I decided that I would only find out if it was true if I tried praying Nicky's prayer in his *Why Jesus?* booklet and asking Jesus to come into my life. So I did pray that prayer. I was sitting at home playing my favourite Van Morrison record when I just got my copy of *Why Jesus?* out and I prayed the prayer at the back, turning away from everything that is wrong, repenting of it and asking God to forgive me and come into my life. It had absolutely no impact upon me whatsoever. So I sort of thought, 'Well great'... Then I went on the Alpha weekend. And then something happened.

I had no idea of the Holy Spirit at that particular time. There was a Welshman, Paul, on the weekend who was what you might call a born-again Christian – seriously filled with the Holy Spirit – who had been cured from being a drug addict when he'd come to Christ. He said to me, "Look, Robert, are you a Christian?" I said, "No." He said, "Well you will be by the end of this weekend." And then he just laughed. He also said, "You realise that the Holy Spirit is hovering over you, don't you? He's going to be with you by the end of the weekend." I thought, 'What on earth is he talking about?' But he kept saying, "Robert, you're going to have a great weekend." And I certainly did.

I listened to the talks and when Nicky asked the Spirit to come amongst us, I prayed for the Spirit to touch me. I felt a real glow and had to sit down. As I sat down, I just started crying – and I couldn't stop. At that moment I knew I had been touched by the Spirit. I had people praying over me.

On the Saturday night, there was a bit of a disco and when the music was beating, all I could hear to the beat of the music was, "Jesus loves you, Jesus loves you." It just wouldn't go away. That night I knew that I had become a Christian. It was 12th November 1994. I will never forget it. Everybody said I was just beaming like a Cheshire Cat for the rest of the weekend.

A couple of days afterwards, I decided to go and tell my wife what had happened. I told her I had become a Christian and that I would like to try to re-build our marriage. She laughed and said, "How on earth could you become a Christian? What have you done to be accepted by God? You will get over it, Robert. This is another one of your crazes like golf and scuba diving and sailing..." I just said, "I knew you would say that. The only way I can convince you is by showing you how I've changed."

Kath thought about it for a week and then phoned me and said, "Well OK. We'll have to go very slowly because the children have been very damaged. What you should do is just come and visit a little bit more regularly." We also agreed that instead of me taking the children away, we would go out together as a family. And that was the starting point of re-building our relationship. Eventually, after building more trust, I moved back to the house just before Christmas. There was still no acceptance at that particular point of time, but following that, throughout the New Year, things slowly built up so that our marriage is, to all intents and purposes, fully restored now.

I think my selfishness has declined considerably and that Kath has started to trust me again. She can see how enthusiastic I am about my faith. As for the children, they think everything is completely fantastic. My little boy was reading the Bible the other day where I had left it on the floor, and he picked it up and said, "Dad, it's a great book this" (he's only seven). "I'm in it not once but twice." He had found the books Samuel 1 and Samuel 2. We go to church every Sunday. Kath did the Alpha Course at our local church. We have joined a Home Group at our local church and I am now getting actively involved in Bible Study.

I now pray every day and read the Bible most days. Now the Lord provides me with the strength to cope with all my difficulties. I know there's no guarantee that everything's going to be rosy in the garden and I don't think it is. But knowing the Lord is there just means so much to me.

Robert and Kath Taylor and their family are now regular attenders of a church near their home in Hertfordshire. Robert also leads a group on the Alpha course at Holy Trinity Brompton.

— oOo —

"My wife ... came back from the service very happy – and I didn't talk to her for about three days."

The story of Nick Sibley

Nick Sibley didn't speak to his wife for three days after she became a Christian. Dogged by financial problems and with a temper aggravated by drink, he finally went to church with her and his attitude to life began to change. Here he tells the story:

In May 1991 my wife became interested in the subject of healing and went along to a free church in Reading which was doing a course on Christian healing. Having spent the last five or six years going to our local church, she suddenly heard about the Holy Spirit for the first time. At that point we lived in a cottage belonging to my father-in-law and that relationship was not easy, so we had a certain amount of pressure on. I put her under a lot of pressure too. I was a difficult person to live with. As a drinker and a smoker, my interests were in other directions. I was very uncaring – shouting at the children and storming about. My aim was common enough – to make money and enjoy spending it while I was young.

I had noticed this change in her, though. When she came back from these meetings she was a lot more relaxed and they were obviously having a good effect on her. After that, she made a Christian commitment at a healing service at the church. She came back from the service very happy – and I didn't talk to her for about three days. I don't know why. I think I was angry. I used to get very annoyed about it because it used to take her away from me on a Sunday morning. Then she started going in the evenings as well.

We went away on holiday and came back to be told to move out of our cottage by her father, which put a lot of additional pressure on us. I am an antique dealer and I didn't have a regular income in the middle of a recession.

About two weeks after that there was another healing service and Heather suggested I go with her to see what happens. This South African evangelist was going to be there. I think I was quite open to it because I'd been written off by my father-in-law, by my bank, and by my doctor who told me I was too old at 32 to play football. I had been thinking, 'What is going on in the world?'

On the day of the service, I was searching through the store where I keep my furniture and found my old school report which described me as "hopeless", "useless" and "will never do any good." So any doubts I had about going were quashed by that! I felt that there must be something better.

So we went off to this service and it was a very

evangelical place which appealed to me at the time. I found it rather exciting. As you walked into the room of about 150 people, just the electricity of, I suppose, the Holy Spirit was there and I knew I was in the right place. Everything the man said that evening spoke to me and, as he encouraged us to worship God, I realised that it was true that Jesus is real.

Then came the time for healing. I had had a bad back for about four or five years which had stopped me playing football and tennis and which was so bad at times that I had to spend two or three days in bed at a time.

I had no idea what was going to happen. The preacher laid his hands on me, prayed, and then asked me to bend over. I bent over and touched my toes which I hadn't done for years. Since that day in September 1991, the pain has gone.

Later on in the evening, someone went up for help with her smoking. She was a chronic addict. He said, "Right hang on. We're going to have a mass prayer for everyone in the room with addictions." About 50 people put their hands up to say they had some kind of addiction. My hand went up. I'd been trying to give up smoking once every five years, and could never do it. So we had this prayer, and I felt nothing.

At the very end he said, "If you want to follow Jesus, you must come up and we'll pray for you." I know my wife was praying I would, so I raised the other hand so she didn't know! About 20 people went up and we followed the prayer he prayed to give our lives to Jesus. That night changed my life. I was so relieved that he's a living God.

I was thinking that if it all ended before 11pm, we could go for a drink in the pub next door. But we finished about 11.05 when all the pubs were shut, so I went back to the car. There were all my cigarettes......and I thought, 'I'll just see what happens'. I left them and the next morning I felt all right and carried on with no withdrawal symptoms. I have never felt the urge to smoke again. I had been on over 30 cigarettes a day before. I used to get the shakes and couldn't speak. It was dreadful. I also kicked my habit for whisky. I could drink about a quarter or half a bottle and now I don't have a taste for it.

Ten days later, we heard through a friend who attends Holy Trinity Brompton that the Alpha course was starting at Malshanger [*Holy Trinity Brompton's conference centre in Hampshire*] 10 days later. And off we both went. We live about 10 miles from Malshanger. I'd never heard any teaching like that before.

I didn't realise that I had been suffering from depression until after becoming a Christian. Then my wife showed me an article from the *Independent on Sunday*. The article was about an author who'd suffered from 'madness' and he'd written an autobiographical account. It was such a catalyst for me – I was in tears for about two days. I suddenly realised it was me. That was happening in the middle of the Alpha course. The Holy Spirit day was coming up, and I was praying that God would make that day really special for me and bring healing to me.

I went through a period of having nightmares which I'd never had before – awful violent nightmares – with someone hitting me over the head with a baseball bat while I was hanging upside down. I was powerless to do anything – at the mercy of some other force. I was praying to be healed of this.

Then, the Friday before the Holy Spirit day, I had this

most wonderful dream. I was taken up to heaven by two silent angels and led into a big white room, completely naked, where God said to me – I assume it was God – "It's not about life on earth. It's about the Resurrection and my Son." That was all that was said. I was standing there before him naked, and bowed, and I said to him, "Do what you want with me, for I am your creation." It was such a healing for me to know that God can take away all these problems. I never had a nightmare again. On the Holy Spirit day, I was filled with the Holy Spirit. It was a great, cleansing joy.

We're much happier now. We almost separated about three years ago when I'd been going through a very bad time trying to get a business going and being very selfish. So it's been a steady claw back.

Since I became a Christian, my sister and brother-in-law have become Christians – and also my cousin, my mother, my stepfather and my niece! My cousin was the first. He lives up north. He phoned me up about six weeks after I'd made a commitment and said, "I hear that something's happened to you. Can it help me?" He was an alcoholic with tremendous family problems. He came down for a weekend and went back with all the Alpha course tapes. He was driving to work one day when he made the commitment to follow Christ.

Nick Sibley and his wife, Heather, continue to attend the church in Reading where they were converted. He says: "Our lives have improved immeasurably and are much more in order – both in our relationships and financially. We now live in a house which more than meets our needs." They have helped to lead a number of Alpha courses.

4

"I was only 24 years old and I didn't want to die."

The story of John Rajah

> *In August 1990 John Rajah was brought to Holy Trinity Brompton by a friend. He was severely ill. He asked for prayer and the next day gave his life to Jesus Christ. Since then remarkable changes have occurred in his life including the healing of a disease which had plagued him for five years. Here he tells the story.*

In 1987 I came to London from our home in Leeds to work for an insurance agency, Allied Dunbar. Soon after my arrival I developed severe pain in my stomach and, after extensive tests, was diagnosed as having Indeterminate Crohn's Colitis, which is an inflammation of the intestines causing, in my case, severe internal bleeding.

I was in hospital for many weeks during the summer of 1988, where I had septicaemia, a very serious infection. I wasn't able to eat or drink and I was fed into my neck through my veins. I'd lost the vision in my left eye and a disc disintegrated in my spine. I felt I was very close to death at that stage and I remember crying out desperately to God.

I was only 24 years old and I didn't want to die. One night I had a vision of two tunnels – a dark tunnel on the left and a dark tunnel on the right with a light at the end of it. I instinctively knew I had to make a choice. I put my foot into the tunnel with the light and hoped for life. After that experience I decided to seek God.

My colon was removed in the Easter of 1989 and I had a bag, which I had to use for about a year and a surgical corset because of my spine, which was quite restrictive.

By now my life had changed completely. I was in constant pain and was hunched like an old man. The doctors do not know what causes this illness and have no cure for it. The surgery was a last resort.

My mother continually spoke of "seeking healing" and one evening in 1990 a Christian friend from my workplace took me to Holy Trinity Brompton where 'healing of the sick' was said to take place. Sandy Millar was preaching and I had a great sense of peace in that place. At the end of the sermon I went forward for prayer and in my heart I prayed to God, "If you want to heal me I know you can, but if I am to be sick I will be. I know you have given me back my life and now I give it to you and leave it all to you." I put my trust in God. Somehow I knew that was the only way to live. After that, I had great peace about my condition.

At that time, I was going to have an operation to remove my colostomy bag, but my surgeon did not want to operate because I was so ill. But I began to feel very much better and decided to have a second medical opinion. I went to hospital for a colonoscopy (an investigation of my colon using a camera) and the test revealed everything to be practically normal with very little bleeding – I still have the pictures. The new surgeons decided they could operate on me and the bag was removed. I felt that God had partially healed me (I was still on a lot of medication). It was too much of a coincidence for any other explanation.

I was encouraged to follow up my commitment to God by attending the Alpha course at the church. I went on the morning course and it was there I finally learned the truth about God. It was like coming in out of the cold. After that moment I was sure that God's hand was at work in my life.

In January 1992, the doctors told me I should try to accept that my condition would not improve and that I would probably have to be on medication for the rest of my life. I was on quite a cocktail of drugs at that time (see table) and was still prone to bleeding and pain.

However God had better plans for my life. On March 18th, 1992, the Alpha talk was on "healing" and the team began to pray for the sick. Two people said that they felt there was someone present with problems regarding their colon and God wanted to heal them.

Jeremy Jennings *[HTB Pastoral Director]* asked if there was anyone present or anybody who knew someone with the disease Colitis to come forward for prayer. I thought "This has got to be me." The members of my Alpha group prayed for me and they had great faith that God would heal me. At that time, I didn't feel any different.

I went home and decided to take a step of faith. I thought, 'I am going to have faith that God has healed

---

JOHN RAJAH'S LIST OF DAILY MEDICATION BEFORE MARCH 1992
Steroids: Prednisolone tablets
Prednisolone suppositories
(and Colifoam enemas)
Painkillers: Co-Proxamol (Distalgesic)
Paracetamol
Anti-diarrhoeals: Immodium or Codeine Phosphate
Antacids: Zantac/Cimetidene/Losec (tried various)
Gaviscon

HOW GOD INTERVENED

Dec 1987:   Perianal abscess and fistula develop requiring surgery.

Summer 1988   Developed diarrhoea with bleeding. Rectal biopsy suggests
              Crohn's disease.
              Taken off all food and water and fed through a drip in the neck.
              Complications of candidal septicaemia with Choroditis (eye
              problem) and later Osteomyelitis of the lumbar spine.

Aug/Sep 1989 Exacerbation of inflammatory bowel disease. Sub-total colectomy
              (most of large bowel removed) with ileo-rectal anastomosis
              (surgical join of small bowel and rectum) and covering loop
              ileostomy (a bypass of the surgical join.)

Dec 1989   Investigatory surgery to assess chances of removal of ileostomy.
              Results not favourable.

Summer 1990   Prayers for healing at Holy Trinity Brompton, giving life to Jesus.

July/Aug 1990 Colonoscopy reveals the gut is 'practically normal'
              The ileostomy was closed on 30.07.90.

Oct 1991   Joins morning Alpha course at HTB. Receives Holy Spirit.
              "It was like coming in out of the cold."

Jan 1992   Physician advises John to be prepared to accept that he may
              always have to be on medication and may never get better and will
              have to tolerate pain.

Mar 1992   Alpha course group prays for healing.
              John comes off all medication for first time in five years.

me and not reach for my medication automatically.' I needed the medication to see me through from one meal to the next without pain or bleeding – and even with it I spent a lot of my time in bed. Even though everybody says this is not recommended, I decided to put aside all my medication and, trusting completely in God's word, prayed in hope. That night, I took one Gaviscon tablet (an antacid) and two Paracetamol for a headache – which, compared to my normal dose of drugs, was like a thimble of water in the sea.

When I woke up the next day there was no pain and I wasn't bleeding! I was unsure of what was going on for a while, (I was even a little scared), but realised God had touched me. From that day on, I became fitter and stronger and no longer depended on the tablets. It was amazing – Jesus healed me and set me free.

It has not meant the end of all my health problems. My back injury began severely playing up in late 1993 and I was finding it difficult to walk. But, after much prayer I was delivered from the pain and was able to walk without a limp again.

The effects of surgery and its consequences from the years of illness are still present but I am not daunted because God has healed me, is still healing me and will continue to heal me.

John Rajah remains a member of Holy Trinity Brompton. He has attended the International Bible Institute of London and in 1994 went on a short-term mission to Sri Lanka. He remains free from his medication, although has recently had some problems with scar tissue caused by the surgical operation to remove his colon in 1989. This has resulted in some spells in hospital. "Anything still wrong with me is all to do with the surgery I underwent," he said. "I am free from the disease, it's just that my colon hasn't grown back – yet!"

— oOo —

"All the people that knew me left me.
I was really, really alone without anybody."

The story of Jaleh MacDonald

Jaleh MacDonald, an Iranian ex-Muslim, tells the remarkable story of how she became a Christian after being healed of a serious, debilitating illness.

In my childhood I had everything. I had a very luxurious life in Iran – a good house, a servant... My father was a General in the Army. He always said to me, "Jaleh, you should grow up and be a good lady. You mustn't lie or steal because you must be good." But I didn't have the power to do all these things.

I was active in a political group in Iran. Then in 1983 I ran away from Iran. I left my family, a good job with an airline, my house, car, everything – I just left it and took six suitcases of clothes and fled to the UK. At that time I was not interested in the Muslim faith, although I grew up in a Muslim family. I did some research about God and other religions. I went to Baha'i, Jewish, Buddhist and other groups because I wanted to know "Who is God?" and why he had created me. I was secretary of a political group in London and a speaker on the radio. But I found myself really under pressure about the question, "Who is God?"

Then an Armenian guy introduced me to an Iranian church in Ealing. I went along and had a good time. I thought it a good place because I could ask all my questions in my own language and they would answer me. But I still had a question mark in my mind. I knew I could continue my research into Christianity and God. I could build up my life and go to college. Then, some 20 days later, I was in Hammersmith College in the canteen waiting to pay for a cup of coffee when suddenly I fell down. They sent me to the hospital. Nobody knows what happened to me. I was happy and talking to people. Then when I woke up I was in Ealing Hospital and for one year and four months I had a terrible time. I was just in and out of hospital. I had a dizziness which meant I had no balance. I couldn't really walk straight. As well as that, the left side of my body had very little sense, particularly my left hand. I was in hospital four times during that time, but all they said to me was they couldn't find anything serious and they didn't know what had happened.

From that time all the people that knew me left me, because they said "She's hopeless. She can't do anything else for us." I was really, really alone without anybody. No support, no money. Sometimes I was really hungry. They still don't know what happened, but one thing I know: it was just an attack of the Enemy. I had only been to the Iranian church the once and because of that I blamed God. I thought this was the punishment from him for going (I had been taught to expect punishment).

Then one night – it was the 24th December – I started to talk to God. It was three o'clock in the morning. I said "God, this is the last time I am going to talk to you. If you are really true and not just the imagination of people, I want to talk to you. I tried to know you through Islam and I found it hopeless, I tried through another religion and found it hopeless. I even tried Jesus but when I went to the church you made me sick. If I want to commit suicide, this is my decision. You can't tell me this is sin. You have done it. If you are really true I want to see you. I want to talk to you."

Then I had a vision in the corner of my room. Even now, when I remember, it was beautiful. I said ... "Are you?" and He said "I am." And I said "I don't believe it, I must touch you." He had a beautiful smile. Then I said "I can't touch you" because my hand didn't have any sense. But he said "You can touch me. I have healed you because I love you." When he said that, I knew in my heart it was Jesus. I started crying and crying.

The next morning I went to church and tested it. Had he healed me or not? I moved my head and I was fine. I tried sitting down and standing quickly – and I was not dizzy. Before, I would have fallen down or something. I had lots of feeling in my hands and body. I said "It is Jesus. He loves me. I understand."

From then on, I went to church every Sunday. After one month, I thought, 'I'm a sinner'. I knew I was a sinner and I must repent and be a new creation because this is the gift of God. He took all my sins. Because of that I really feel humble in my heart to him. I said to him "Forgive me. I accept you. My life is in your hands."

From that time he started to heal me of the things I had lost in my life, in Iran, and the hurt I felt. That healing started emotionally. He taught me that it is the spiritual life that is important, not the life in this world. It doesn't matter how much money I have.

He has called me to evangelism. Whether it is with my boss, or when I go shopping or to my neighbour, I give my testimony to people. I know lots of people that have come to Christ.

One day, a few years later, I was walking past Holy Trinity Brompton on my way to do some shopping. The Lord said "Go inside and I want to give you blessing, Jaleh." I said "Thank you, Lord." I came in and saw Nicky Gumbel, who invited me on the Alpha course. It was here that God gave me a better understanding about the Christian life and gave me a stronger foundation for my faith.

Jaleh has now married and she and her husband, Andrew MacDonald, attend a Baptist church near their home. They are helping with an Alpha course at the church.

— oOo —

"They found problems and said, 'It's virtually impossible for you to have a child...'"

The story of Karl Davies

Karl Davies is married with two children. Disabled by the Thalidomide drug, he has shortened arms. Here he tells how his life has been dramatically changed through coming to know the love of Jesus Christ through the Alpha course and prayer.

I used to go to church as a Cub Scout – it was called 'church parade'. I was about eight years old and I really disliked it because I had to get up early. No-one in my family went to church. I had always prayed the desperation-type prayers like "Oh God, please help me out of this one", but nothing much more. When Joanna and I were planning to get married in 1987, we had to do the compulsory business of going to church for 'n' months to show commitment and to hear the banns read. It was a quite a stuffy, formal church. The congregation was mostly elderly and people kept their overcoats on, had their handbags on their laps and hardly ever spoke to anybody.

But the more I sat there listening to sermons, the more I thought, 'Something is making sense to me here.' I felt as though there was a godly presence at church. We got married and kept on going to church. Then Jo felt she didn't want to keep going because she didn't agree with the vicar's views on the ordination of women. So we stopped going. I kept trying to insist, but it was causing hassle.

A few years went by and we decided to try to have a family – to no avail. We went to the doctor and she suggested some tests. She found problems and referred me for specialist help. When they tested me at the Royal Free Hospital, they confirmed the problems and said, "It's virtually impossible for you to have a child unless you've got a lot of money and can go private with IVF [in-vitro fertilisation]." They made it clear there was virtually no chance – even with IVF. So they told us to consider adopting. We approached the council but they said no because I was disabled. They said, "These children have got enough problems to deal with in life being adopted without having a disabled father to boot as well." We were quite knocked back by this.

All through this time, Jo didn't know I was praying. I've always been a self-contained person and don't share everything (or I didn't anyway). I found feelings and things like that very hard to talk about. I knew to whom I was praying, but I was very ignorant about the Christian faith. For example, I didn't even realise then that it was an historical fact that Jesus ever existed!

Fostering was something we had always wanted to do as well, so we phoned up and asked to be considered as foster carers. We were told that would be OK if we came on a 10-week intensive course for potential foster carers. So we went along and started going down that route. All this time I was praying for Jo to become pregnant. We got through the course, were approved and our first foster placement was authorised.

A day later our foster child, a four-year-old boy called Arron, arrived. Two days later, to our amazement, Jo discovered she was pregnant! My prayers had definitely been answered. Arron was with us the whole time Jo was pregnant and, during that time, he came up for adoption. But we weren't allowed to apply to adopt him because Jo was pregnant and you're not allowed to apply to adopt if you are pregnant until your own child has been born – in case your feelings change. I was praying for things to be delayed long enough so we could adopt Arron. In the end, it all came right and Alex was born and we were approved soon afterwards to adopt Arron.

I said my prayers of thanks and I said to Jo that I would like to start going to church again. It made sense as we wanted our children christened as well, and we decided to go back to our local church where we were married. The vicar tried to convince me to become confirmed before the children's christening, and I agreed to think about it.

Another problem was that Alex had been born deaf. I

realised the first day he was born because as I was talking to him in his cot and there was just no reaction at all. I mentioned it to my father in law, who clicked his fingers right by Alex's head in the hospital. There was absolutely no response. At home we would leave his Moses' basket right next to the telephone and it didn't disturb him at all. So I did what I had always done in circumstances like this and I prayed again. It was amazing really. He went to hospital and he had tests and they said he had no hearing at all. The specialist said that in a few years time there was a chance that some (limited) hearing would develop. I was still praying but Jo was still not aware of any of it. Then one Sunday morning in church, I had a strong feeling that I should talk to Alex. I looked down at him in his basket and I said 'Alex'. And he heard me and looked up at me. I am sure that that was the first time he heard anything at all. At his next check, they found a dramatic change in the development of his hearing. Now he has virtually perfect hearing.

There had been times when I had wondered if all the answers to my prayers had just been coincidence. But this was the final moment when I felt God said: "Look, I am here. I have done this and I did those other things." I then wondered what I should do.

I work in the computer industry and at this point someone at work invited me to HTB for a service. I was just amazed at how different it was. Everyone was so friendly and there was a real atmosphere of praise and joy in worship which is what I had been looking for but missed.

In July 1992 the same colleague, now a friend, invited me to HTB's Reunion '92, where all the church plants came together in Methodist Central Hall, Westminster, for a celebration. Eric Delve spoke about Christ's death, and what it had achieved. I came out on cloud nine deciding to become a confirmed Christian, which I did – through my local church, just three weeks later!

We began to visit HTB more regularly, and people started saying, "Why not do the Alpha Course?" And they started telling me what the Alpha Course was. They said "It will change your life and you won't be the same again", which both challenged and intrigued me. You see, at this point I had a faith, but only a little knowledge with little understanding. So I did the course. Jo didn't come because we live near Luton, but since I worked in London it was easy for me to get to. The course made real sense to me. For the second and third weeks, we went to Greece on holiday and I took the tapes. On the Wednesday when I should have been at Alpha I was lying on the beach listening to the tape.

Then I went on the Alpha weekend at Chichester. That really was the turning point for me. On the Friday night before I went to bed, I said, "Dear God, please help me to enjoy the weekend and to get through it all. I really want to know you and want to commit my life to your will."

That night I had the most horrific nightmare. I was being chased by a pack of killer dogs across fields. I woke up in a cold sweat and had a very bad night's sleep. The next day, when Nicky was talking about the fact that there is nothing that you have done which you can't be forgiven for, I began to think about my past. I had been part of a 'Circle' in my younger days where we read Tarot Cards and I still had Tarot Cards in the house and books on Tarot, which Jo hadn't wanted to be there for years but I had insisted that I wanted to keep them. One of the images was that I should clear all these things out and throw them away – and turn my back on all the Tarot business and renounce it.

Another concerned the fact that I wasn't currently speaking to my father. There were things wrong in the relationship there. And there were a whole series of things which I knew I had to put right. At the end of the talk, the Holy Spirit was invited to come and I felt a really intense glowing sensation. At the point of repentance I got a series of images in my mind about the things that were wrong in my life which I had to put right before I could fully become a Christian and accept the gospel. And I repented of all of them. I felt I had been forgiven for everything I'd ever done in the past – a total release from all my burdens. It made me break down and I sat down and cried. It was the only way I could express anything at the time. It was all I could do.

I followed the prayer Nicky suggested word for word. I thanked God for his son Jesus Christ; I repented of everything in the past; I asked for forgiveness and invited Jesus Christ into my life. I finally knew that I was a Christian. It made me feel as if I just wanted to walk around with a great big beaming smile on my face. I came home after church on the Sunday night of that same weekend and I started throwing out everything I could find that connected me in any way with the Tarot business.

I've now sorted things out with my father too and we all get on very well and he comes up and he sees his grandchildren. In fact, I have sorted out everything from that sequence of visions and I'm much much happier for it. The Lord is totally in control now.

I now know that it just doesn't matter how large or how small the subject of your prayer – because, after all, everything is insignificant when you compare it to running a universe – your prayers are listened to and answered. I also know that things only happen when God knows they are right for you. If all my prayers had been answered the way I wanted in the past, my life wouldn't have followed the same course. Now, my prayers are much more of a conversation. It's almost as though I discuss things when I am praying and I know an interaction is taking place. I also read the Bible much more. Before, I hardly used it at all.

Jo was amazed at what an impact the weekend had had on me. She noticed that I was calmer, happier and altogether a much nicer person. The temper was under control, and I was under control, because someone else was in control.

People have said to me in work that I am much more approachable now and easier to work with. I now know that nothing can happen to me without the permission of the Father. It has also helped me talk about emotions and feelings. I'm a much more open person and can talk about things which I've previously found very difficult.

I prayed with my group at the Alpha weekend that Jo would do the Alpha course. I didn't feel she had a relationship with Jesus at that time. Now she has listened to the complete course on tape and recently we both went on an Alpha weekend together. Jo used to listen to the tapes while she was doing her ironing, and she found them really enjoyable. That really completed it for her. Now she prays and reads the Bible every day after she has put the children to bed.

I don't see my physical situation as a disability because it doesn't really disable me from doing anything – apart from changing a light bulb and things like that. It's only visibly being very different. I find that people stare occasionally, but I just don't worry about that at all.

My parents have helped me a great deal during the growing up and formative years in dealing with it positively and making me do things. It's never worried me. It's not something I've needed to pray about or needed help with. But I actually find it easier now knowing the extent Jesus suffered for us and what he went through. Because of the suffering he did for us, it makes him supremely qualified to be a counsellor. I share all my problems with him now.

Karl and Joanna Davies are now members of Holy Trinity Brompton, where Karl is a group leader on the Alpha course. They are members of one of the church's home groups.

"You came to my rescue, Lord, and saved my life."
Lamentations 3:58

5

"I was thrown into a pit of despair...
Nothing could lift me. I was so, so sad."

The story of Derek and Francie Lygo

> *When Derek and Francie Lygo's three-month-old
> daughter Chloe was a victim of cot death in 1991,
> their world fell apart. Here Francie, who gave
> birth to their second daughter Freya in 1993, tells
> the story of what happened and how a new-found
> relationship with God has changed both their lives:*

I've always been brought up in the Christian tradition.
Derek was an atheist but we were married in church.
We were engaged within two weeks of meeting each
other and it was love at first sight. We still love each
other, probably even more than we loved each other
then, if that's possible.

Ever since I was a child, I have always felt that there
would be a time in my life when I would get to know
God better. I didn't know when that would be but I knew

it would be sometime. I don't think thoughts like that had ever even occurred to Derek. Life when we were married was going very well: he had a very good job in the City and we were on the crest of a wave. It hadn't always been easy but we were very, very happy.

Then I became pregnant with Chloe which was the fulfilment of our dreams. We had wanted a baby as soon as we were married. We were thinking of moving into a bigger house, gearing up the mortgage. I did not have an easy pregnancy and I was very ill in hospital for about six weeks before her birth. But Chloe was born and she was a lovely, bouncy, happy baby and everything was wonderful.

Nothing, nothing in the world could have prepared us for what was going to happen next. It was November 26, 1991, in the evening, that she stopped breathing. It was a moment of distraction: Derek was on the phone, I was cooking supper, and when I went to look at her a few minutes later, I found her and she was dead. Derek called an ambulance and we attempted to revive her before it came. Eventually it arrived and she was raced to St George's Hospital, Tooting, where she was put in Intensive Care.

It was awful when they were trying to get her heart going. It took a long time, probably about forty-five minutes, and a human being dies in three minutes if they don't get oxygen. So that in itself was amazing, that after forty-five minutes they were able to start her heart beating again. She was put on a life support machine and never breathed on her own again. She lived another seventeen hours, and they were the longest hours in my life. A second seemed like a day, a minute seemed like a year and an hour seemed like eternity. We didn't know what to do with ourselves. There are no words that can describe parents' feelings. She was our life. One minute we had a bouncy, healthy baby and the next minute the person our whole lives revolved around was dying. Our lives came to a grinding halt. We were unprepared and numb. We wanted to be with her, but the agony of seeing her was almost too much to bear. We were sick with shock and exhausted beyond belief. We had done everything for her in the past but now we found ourselves helpless and other people had taken over. We could not just pick our baby up, walk out of that place and give her a cuddle which we longed to do. Everything was alien to us and it was a struggle to take it in.

But it was in this situation that the Lord showed his compassion, which was amazing. I had always wanted Chloe christened. Before she became ill Derek was indifferent to it and he hadn't wanted a big fuss but now he agreed and we decided she had to be christened. Gradually it became obvious that we were going to lose her and as our hopes for her life faded we realised it was an ordeal we would have to live through. The chaplain was there and we had her christened. Moments after she was christened I said to Derek, "The Holy Spirit's here!" and I didn't know anything about the Holy Spirit. God's love for me was so incredible that he sent his Spirit down to comfort me at that time. I felt this amazing source of strength and peace.

Towards the end our nurse said she thought I should hold Chloe. I was frightened I'd hurt her. Then she said, "I think she'd far rather be in your arms." So I did, and she died in my arms. But before that happened, I felt God. I felt overwhelmed with his love and I felt held in his arms, as I was holding Chloe in mine. And the extraordinary thing is that I didn't really know that any of these things could happen. I wasn't a proper Christian at all, apart from going through the traditional motions, and yet that's when I knew that I'd had a physical experience of his love and light. There were tears, but no hysteria. The calmness came from him. I felt I had no right to hold her back and though my heart was breaking as I held her little hand I knew with certainty she was with Jesus and that Jesus himself had been longing to hold and care for her.

Then we left the hospital and we came home and we had no child. I was thrown into a pit of despair and my world was black: it was like I was being suspended in a well of black ink. All around there was suffocating blackness; I couldn't look out of a window and feel joy as part of me had died. Nothing could lift me. I was so, so sad.

We went to Florida for Christmas as had been planned. When we came back, I bumped into Susie Farley, a neighbour I had met at ante-natal classes. Of course I had no baby, and her little baby Harry was there and she asked where Chloe was, and I had to tell her. She was so kind. She was obviously very sad and asked me if I was a Christian. My words to her were that I didn't know if I was if God could do such things, yet all the time I knew I'd experienced his love. Susie asked me if I'd think of going to Alpha, a course at her church, Holy Trinity Brompton. I wouldn't have gone if she hadn't driven me there and introduced me to Deirdre, Lorna and others. But the extraordinary thing was that the moment my foot walked over the threshold of the room there, I felt the same feeling of light and joy and love that I'd felt at the time of Chloe's death.

I never looked back after that moment. That was the only thing that lifted me. I went back again and completed the course. People were so kind. I suddenly knew there was the sky and there were birds in it and there was a rainbow and wonderful things around. There was something worth living for again. Derek couldn't believe the difference in me. He was very suspicious because he thought I was getting involved in some Moonie religious organisation and he thought he had to stamp it out fast. I managed to persuade him to come on the next evening Alpha course. Very sweetly he said he'd come for me. For the first five weeks he was aggressive and had convincing arguments against becoming a Christian.

Then one day, half way through the course, he was sitting in the barber shop and looking at himself, and he prayed that God would come into his life. He now says that God answered immediately. He says the most amazing feeling was that he felt the whole of the heavens rejoice as though a voice was saying "At long last! We've been waiting all your life for you to do this. Thank you for doing it!"

Our lives changed dramatically after that point. Derek resigned from his job, so we had almost a year together while he was unemployed. The Bible talks about putting you in a spacious place and God did. He gave us the space we needed to be ourselves and to build our faith. He has more than provided for us in every possible way. We've never had to worry about anything. He has also provided us with wonderful friends, far closer than we've ever had before, who pray for all parts of our lives consistently – our home group, my wives' group and other Christian friends. In the same week that our second child, Freya was born, Derek got the job he's in now which is perfect for him. It was such a clear demonstration of God's perfect timing for our lives.

Every day I cry for Chloe. I still love her. Some months after she died I did ask the question 'Why?' because she seemed so perfect and it seemed such a waste. You always know when it's God replying because the answer is so amazing. I sensed him say, "Chloe is much happier in heaven than she would ever have been on earth." And I said, "But I loved her so much, Lord. There was so much that I wanted to teach her, so much I wanted to show her." He said to me, "Now do you understand why you need to love me at least as much as you love Chloe, there is so much I want to teach and show you."

Little Freya is the most lovely child and we delight in her. As Freya grows up we see how much she would have loved to have had her sister. She adores other children. Grief is not something you 'get over' like a bad cold and the pain is something you learn to live with; it's the physical missing of the person you love which is the hardest thing to bear. But the Lord continues to be our strength. He has never yet failed. He continues in his Spirit to heal and comfort us and we always arrive at a restored peacefulness once more. There is no secret to knowing his love, we only have to seek it. Through Chloe's death I knew what 'it' was all about and that in suffering I was growing up, literally overnight. Growing up is learning to accept God's will. This for me was the moment of reckoning. I felt I had only half-lived. My spirit has been awakened and this was an aspect to my existing on this earth which I had never known before.

The Lord must not only have loved me beyond my understanding but I think he knew that once I knew and loved him, I would never turn back his power on my life and my family. It has been too strong a force. I will never forget his goodness to me in my darkest hours. I was nothing before him and I would be nothing without him – he is the centre of my life.

Derek and Francie Lygo have now moved to a village in Lincolnshire, where they help with Alpha courses at the local church where they are members. Their third daughter, Sophie, was born in September 1995. Francie says, "When I look back at where we were after Chloe's death I can see that the Lord has certainly and so gently restored us. We have come a long way since the black pit of despair and grief. God has been constant in his goodness."

— oOo —

"I had been living my life in a dark hole ..."

The story of Rosalie Ryder

Rosalie Ryder's life was one of heartbreak, violence and despair – but she never gave up hope that there was a God who could help her. Then came a telephone call from a friend who told her about a course in Christianity he was going on. This is her story:

I grew up in an atmosphere that was fairly turbulent. My mother was very domineering and my father enjoyed a good drink every night – which created heated arguments between him and my mother. My mother used to pray to God to get my father to stop drinking and smoking and gambling – and from turning into an alcoholic. I remember my brother taking me to Sunday School and thoroughly enjoying it, but, even though I had a belief in God and Jesus, I never really understood what I was being taught about them. At the age of 16 my Dad began to take me into the pub where he drank and that was the beginning of my downfall. I began drinking Babychams and cider, and I too got the taste for a little tipple.

Then one evening (by now I was 17), a friend of my brother's, called Barry, took a fancy to me and began to chat me up. He gained my trust and I began to feel safe with him. Until one fateful night when he invited me back on my own. For the first time in my life I was totally drunk and falling down. He began to maul me. I was crying and begging him to stop. He totally ignored me and took away my virginity. I was absolutely devastated. I felt degraded, filthy. I'd always wanted to save myself for the person I married. Now I felt unclean and that I was no good for anyone else. There and then, subconsciously, I gave myself to this man – as I felt I wasn't fit for anyone else. I also found out that he was a married man, but his wife had gone to Spain for a year to work. I was so naive. He and his sister and friends smoked dope and I was always left out of the jokes. I felt shut out and very lonely. Several times he two/three-timed me. I always forgave him and carried on with him.

Then his wife came back and he told me we were finished as they were going to give it another go. I was totally shattered. I had truly believed their relationship was over. It was about this time that I found out I was pregnant. He was going to pay for an abortion, but before the day of my abortion, I miscarried. A month or so afterwards he came to me saying his marriage to his wife was truly over and they were now getting a divorce so we could see each other again. I went back with him. My 'A' levels went totally out of the window and I didn't take the exams. I was now a very heavy drinker and smoker and was taking drugs.

Barry threw me over a couple more times for other girls – and now I found myself trying to sleep with other men, to try to hurt him like he was hurting me. I was gradually sinking lower and lower, stripping my self esteem and self respect with each action of deprivation. One last time Barry ended it with me. Again I was just pregnant – and again, with all the emotional stress I was under, I miscarried. After a week or so he said he wanted me back but this time he would marry me. Well that did it for me – the magic word 'marriage'. I would marry the man who took away my virginity after all. By now I was 20 and I thought all the pain and anguish I had suffered because of him would soon be worth it. We got married. I didn't feel 100% sure on the day, but I thought I had to go through with it. By now he had even begun to hit me.

We had only been married a few months when he decided we would be landlord and lady of a public house. So we moved away from my family and friends and my nursing career to a pub in Gloucester. I was very lonely now. He didn't like any of the punters to know I was his wife and became aggressive if I kissed him on the cheek or cuddled him. I soon found out that he was sleeping not only with the barmaids but some of the punters too.

My next move was to leave Barry and I arranged to run off with a male punter. I told Barry and it was then that he gave me the worst beating of all. He snapped the tendon in my right arm, leaving my whole arm useless. I was bruised from head to toe where he just thumped and kicked me.

Eventually Barry and I talked. He promised not to hit me any more and we decided to give it another go. In that period I tried for a baby, thinking a baby would seal our union. He ignored me the whole of my pregnancy – still going off with other women. Then, when the baby was born, he went on a lads-only holiday. I was absolutely shattered. He had also started beating me again. I decided then I couldn't live like this. I began seeking help from a solicitor and just after Christopher was a year old my solicitor had Barry served with a writ to leave the house and not to touch me again. He was very angry, but he left.

It was then that I prayed my first prayer since meeting Barry. I asked God to help me. Once he left home I proceeded to act cheap. I had a friend who would come out with me and we'd get thoroughly drunk and chat up all the guys. I began to pray to God, "Please God send me someone I can love as much as they love me, who'll be really nice to me."

After about four months someone who I'd known briefly came back into my life. He was an electrician and came to do an electrical job for me. We began dating and I realised just what a wonderful person he was. Paul and I saw each other every day. After Paul and I had dated for a year we began to make plans to marry. He belonged to a scouts group and was a leader. That year in July his group planned to go to Kenya for one month. We were to get married in September. I didn't want him to go because I needed him to be with me. Because he went I felt he didn't really love me after all. Then something snapped and I felt I had to hurt Paul because he had hurt me. So I was unfaithful to him. Three weeks before the wedding, I told Paul what I had done and why I'd done it. I said I didn't deserve him and to cancel the wedding. So I packed up and left Paul in Gloucester while I went to London.

I then spent the next three months getting thoroughly drunk. I'm sure I was turning into an alcoholic. But still Paul kept on being kind and patient. Then one night something clicked. In my drunken stupor, something told me that I really loved Paul and needed to be with him. From that day on I never touched another drink. He wanted to wait six months before deciding on another wedding date. In those six months I had to go to see a hypno-psychotherapist, who helped me a great deal. Then we found out my Dad was dying of cancer of the lungs. We brought the wedding forward and my Dad gave me away, but he died soon afterwards. Again, I was devastated.

At that time, Paul was in a job he hated and I found myself praying to God again to please send Paul a job he would enjoy doing. God answered my prayers again and some friends of ours offered us a business opportunity. It was a business that kept on mentioning people's success was due to God. It was a good, ethical, moral, sincere business. For a short time, I began going to the local church and my darling Paul bought me a *Living Bible* for Mother's Day. I began to read the Old Testament slowly. But I stopped. It was going straight over my head.

And then one day, two years later, I received a phone call from a friend who told me about the Alpha course. It was a friend called Lee Duckett, a telephone engineer, who said he'd been to a church called Holy Trinity Brompton and heard about something called an Alpha

Course which was an introduction to Christianity. I said, "That sounds really great, Lee. Can you keep me informed?" And inside I suddenly thought, 'YES! This could be what I've been waiting for for years.' Something just clicked inside me. I just thought, 'This is the avenue back to God that I've been waiting for.' While the course was going on, I was ringing Lee every day. He sounded so excited about it all. I thought, 'Yes, that's what I want. I need this.'

At the end of the course, Paul and I could see the difference in Lee. Although he had always tried to be cheerful and crack jokes, his eyes were just dead really. And then all of a sudden it was like the light started shining in them. I said, "Lee, I've got to do what you're doing." Later we started an Alpha course at HTB.

All those years of feeling utterly desolate, utterly unclean and ashamed, riddled with guilt and not believing I deserved forgiveness but longing for it, were all soon to end. Doing the course meant travelling to London from Gloucester on Wednesday and staying with my mother and then leaving very early the following morning. I enjoyed Alpha so much I just didn't want to leave. I thought, 'Yes. This is what I've been looking for for *such* a long time'.

We went away for the Alpha weekend and it was the most amazing weekend I think I've ever experienced – so warm and so loving. God began his healing on me. I asked for laughter and I got floods of tears. But I had begun to inch my way back through the pain and anguish I had been living with. I can now look on my ex-husband as a human being in his own right and not as this monster that I had implanted in my head. After Alpha, I wrote him a letter saying that I forgave him and I hoped that he could forgive me – because obviously you only look at situations from your own perspective.

I had been living my life in a dark hole. I was carrying a great weight on my shoulders. That burden has gone and I am filled with great hope, joy, excitement and love, and all I want to do is to serve Christ in whatever form he chooses. I love Jesus with all my heart.

Paul and Rosalie Ryder are now regular attenders of a church in Cheltenham, Gloucestershire. Rosalie says, "I see my life as a jigsaw puzzle that in my early days God helped to piece together. When I shut God out of my life the puzzle was almost destroyed. Since I have turned to God again, I have allowed him to help me put the pieces back into place. Every now and again as the puzzle has grown, I have thought, "Thanks, God. I can take it from here", and I have begun to put the wrong piece into the wrong place, slowing my progress considerably. But God is patient and kind and healing – and I am slowly building back the puzzle. I love to read the word of God nightly and, as God heals me, I have far more hope for tomorrow."

"From every part of the world they will turn to him."
Psalm 22:27

6

"I have been attending church for more than 40 years and nothing like this has ever happened."

The story of Tony Summers

Australian businessman Tony Summers came to Holy Trinity for the first time in 1991 to attend the wedding of his son Hamish. Later, he began to listen to tapes of sermons by HTB curate Nicky Gumbel during car journeys around his home in Adelaide, Australia where his wide business interests included clothing manufacture, food production, high technology, finance, property and rural enterprises. He also held several community positions including an influential role as Warden of the Cathedral and Chairman of the Adelaide Festival of Art. After listening to the tapes almost every day, in 1992 he gave his life to Jesus Christ. Here he tells the story:

We've got a flat just across the road from the Brompton Oratory. We used to stay there for very brief visits to London. Then Hamish, my eldest son, moved to London to work for me there and he met a young lady, who lived round in Thurloe Square. About a year later, he announced his engagement and another year later they were married at Holy Trinity Brompton, because that was the local parish church.

Before the marriage on 19 July 1991 we went to a Sunday service there in the morning. I saw the excitement of the place and the way people were singing and there was an excellent sermon which I understood.

On the wedding day, though, something really happened. We came into the church. It was a very formal type of gathering. The families of both sides were from rather formal backgrounds. We were in the front row, my wife, Kit, and I, and then Nicky Gumbel let forth on 1 Corinthians 13 and he spoke about Hamish and Harriet and put their names in the text. Kit and I were overwhelmed about this. We looked at each other and we said, "He's talking about Kit and Tony." What he was saying about them seemed to apply to us. "This is too much," we said.

At the reception and subsequently a lot of people – young and old, Australians, English, from about five continents – said they were just overwhelmed by Nicky's sermon. I was quite affected by the sermon and we looked at each other and said "What's happening with our marriage?" It was quite moving. It wasn't just the emotion of my son being married, it was what Nicky was saying.

I returned to Australia, but found myself back in England two weeks later on business. I went back to Holy Trinity and heard another sermon. Kit came with me. Afterwards we went downstairs and Kit picked up a tape called 'Is Life Worth Living?'. I was quite horrified by that because I thought, 'Why would she wonder, "Is life worth living?" I've given her everything for the last

30 years – I don't think I want to listen to that'. We brought the tape home and one day she was listening to it, and said "You might like to listen to this". Some weeks later I put it in my car and as I was driving I switched the tape on. He talked about Malcolm Muggeridge and the old man and the young man in the Ecclesiastes story and particularly the verse, "Yet when I surveyed all that my hands had done and what I had toiled to achieve, everything was meaningless, a chasing after the wind".

I thought, 'This Gumbel fellow's doing it to me again – he's talking about me. He talked about me at my son's wedding and now he's talking about me on this tape.' It just seemed to fit me. I took it right to heart. I've listened to that tape more than 20 times since that day. Then I wrote to him in about November 1991 and said, "Look, this tape has been fantastic. It really has helped me. It made me stop in my tracks from building companies. Have you got any more?" I enclosed some money but I was overwhelmed with what came back, because I got the full Alpha course, the Sermon on the Mount and another dozen tapes of various talks. That was really like a gift from Heaven for us. We took them with us at Christmas time to our station property in the outback and I just went from one to the other. We listened to them constantly and they seemed to have a real message for us. There is a theme through them. There is humour through them. There is a message that comes through crystal clear.

The consequence is that we've changed our direction here. I'm still semi-involved with the Cathedral, but I'm no longer Warden. We go to Holy Trinity Church here in Adelaide, a church similar to Holy Trinity Brompton. It's the only one like it in Adelaide.

Then a most amazing thing happened last Sunday. In life you have periods when there's pressure commercially and it's not plain-sailing. We'd been under pressure – and all our five children had gone. Hamish is back in London, Nigel's going to Paris shortly to live, Joshua's at school in another State, even our youngest one, Magnus, (aged six) had gone to Melbourne for a week with Caroline.

We were coming back from Adelaide airport on Sunday night. I'd put a tape of Nicky's called 'True Freedom' in my pocket, in case we wanted to listen to it on the way back (I carry one in my pocket all the time.) The lights were on in Holy Trinity. It was after 7pm and the service had been under way for about 15 minutes. I said "There are the lights, why don't we stop?" So we went in and we just got there in time as the senior minister of the church, Reg Piper, was getting up to speak. It was a Sunday night service, packed full of university types and young people. The songbooks were out and it's very electric. The Spirit's really working, you can just feel it in the air. He got up and spoke on 'Freedom in Christ' – exactly the same thing that Nicky was talking about on his tape – and we looked at each other. I pulled this tape out of my pocket and said "'True Freedom' – that's exactly the same subject".

He gave a talk which was not dissimilar to Nicky's talk – the same basic facts: freedom from bondage, which I'd never understood. After the service (there were 800 people in the place), he got out of the pulpit (we were on a back row on the side) and he appeared behind us. He put his head between us and he said "Well, how are things going?" We looked at him in amazement! How did he get there, and how was he talking to us? I said "Look what I've had in my pocket and listened to coming home tonight." I pulled out the freedom tape of Nicky's.

After the Communion that Sunday night, 26th April 1992, I prayed "Jesus, I've opened my heart, will you please come in and fill me with the Holy Spirit."

I know that is exactly what he did because it was striking. It was evident. The presence was there. My wife had an experience at the same time. On one of these tapes Nicky says he became a Christian 24 hours after Nicky Lee. Well, Kit and I can say that we met Christ genuinely within the same hour.

Now we are free of the bondage that Nicky was talking about and we'll never be the same again. We are absolutely free. We are only answerable to God.

I went to my office and the way I handled the meetings, even on day one, was different. My marriage has never been better!

I have been attending church for more than 40 years and nothing like this has ever happened. It's the most extraordinary experience of my entire life.

Tony Summers has now realigned his world-wide business interests and moved to London with his family. He is actively involved in Christian community work and ministry in central London. Here, he has studied at the Institute of Contemporary Christianity and the International Bible College of London, from where he graduated in 1995 with the Higher Diploma of Ministry. All five of his children have become active Christians during the last three years. Tony said, "My life-sustaining scripture verse these days is Philippians 4:4 which says, "Rejoice in the Lord always. I say it again, rejoice!"

— oOo —

"We were brought up to believe that if you do wrong, there are 18 dungeons into which you fall ..."

The story of Ginny Quay

> *In May 1993 Ginny Quay and her husband David were baptised at Holy Trinity Brompton. Here she tells how an upbringing where she was taught to believe in many gods has given way to a relationship with Jesus Christ:*

I was brought up in a family in Penang, Malaysia, and our religion was a kind of Buddhism plus Taoism. In the Buddhist way of life, you have to be kind to people, but in Taoism you have hundreds and hundreds of gods. If you see a tree with a strange shape, there is obviously a god there. There are cow gods; gods that eat opium; gods of all kinds.

When I was 10 or 11 I went to my grandmother in another town for the holidays, and I had a high fever. She took me to a temple and she prayed to an idol. Then she visited a medium who went into a trance and started writing something which was meant to make me feel better. Then we went home and performed a ritual ceremony cutting the air with a meat cleaver and chanting. Then she had to burn a strip of paper up and mix the ashes in a glass with water and then drink it down. When I was better a couple of days later, she bought some opium from a shop which she stuck on the tongue of another idol.

My brother would visit mediums quite regularly because he was often sick. Every time you walk past a house in Malaysia, you can see an idol at the front or back of the house. We had five idols in the living room and one in the kitchen.

One of my aunts is a Christian, and she tried to take us to church now and then, but because my granny was so against it we were barred from going to church. Christianity was not considered good for you, because every time a Christian does wrong, he can say, "Please forgive me," and that's it. We were brought up to believe that if you do wrong, there are 18 dungeons into which you fall. Whatever you do, every dungeon you go down, you will be punished accordingly when you die. There is no escape, no forgiveness. That was really scary when I was a child, because as children we sometimes did lie and we believed we were going down dungeons.

We were not supposed to go to my aunt's house, and not supposed to talk about Jesus Christ in our house. When we saw church people coming, we had to run to our door and close it. If they came knocking, we'd say, "Go away, we don't like you" or "We'll set our dogs on you!"

When I was 19 years old, waiting for some exam results, I was working temporarily in an office and a friend said, "Would you like to come to church with us?" I said, "No, I don't believe any of that." But one thing I did like doing was singing, and when I asked what they did there, she said, "We sing songs." So I did go along and we started singing hymns, and the wording was so meaningful, that I found that having gone once, I wanted to go always. In the end I found myself asking, "Why can't I? What's wrong with it?" So I started going to prayer meetings and on Sundays, but only if my aunt – another aunt, who was my guardian – didn't know about it. It was tormenting me and I was thinking,

"What am I going to do?" This was something good – so very different from the way I was brought up.

Then one night when I went to sleep, I just prayed to the one God that is the highest of all. I said, "I'm in search of someone, some peace, something that doesn't scare me when I go to a temple and see idols and people going in trances and doing weird things like that – because it's really scary." So I said, "I would like to know you."

I still didn't tell my aunt, but I kept going to church and gradually came to realise that the "highest of all" was Jesus, although I was still very confused. I'd be thinking, "I'm so useless – who am I that he can actually love me so much?"

I married at the age of 25, having met my husband in Kuala Lumpur where I had gone to work. His name is David Quay. He didn't believe in Christianity. I tried to introduce my husband to Christ but every time I did that there was a row between us.

Every Sunday morning I would say a prayer before I touched him to wake him up, saying, "Lord, can you make him come to church with me". The amazing thing was that most of the time it worked! He would say, "Oh all right then, let's go." That was how I came to know that prayers do work.

We came to England in 1985 because my husband was studying law. After we arrived, I went looking for a church, and I found a church called 'Seventh Day Adventist'. That ended up putting even more questions in my mind. They asked, 'Why do people go to church on Sunday when it's supposed to be Saturday?' and 'Why do people celebrate Christmas on December 25 when it's not his birthday?' I was so confused that I decided I didn't want to belong to any church any more.

I wanted to be a Christian – just me and God. So I didn't go to church any more. I did some correspondence Bible studies instead. Then we had a baby girl.

After that I started working at the Science Museum and at that stage David started asking questions. He would say, "Who is God?" And I prayed and tried to answer. One Sunday evening we were walking through Knightsbridge to catch a bus to go back to Finsbury Park when we saw a sign which said "6.30pm Informal service."

It was August 26 1993, and I'd finished working at 6pm and my husband had met me, so we were walking past Holy Trinity at about 6.15pm. So we crept in right at the back and it was lovely. I was in tears! My husband liked it too so the next Sunday we came... and the next Sunday... and we have been coming ever since.

One evening I went up to the receptionist and said that I would like to get baptised. So the receptionist said, "Fill out this form, come on the Alpha Course and then come back to us and we'll baptise you." Alpha was brilliant! I was the first person there every week! And my husband started buying books and Bibles after Bibles! He's got a dictionary of the Bible too – and all the tapes of Alpha because he couldn't make it to some because he was studying. So what he did was to buy the whole package and Nicky Gumbel's book *Questions of Life*. Every time he read a chapter, he said to me, "This is actually true! This is good. It explains exactly what I want to know."

Finally, my husband said to me, "That's it. I will accept Christianity. There's no other god that I would go to. This is going to be our family's religion for the rest of our lives."

So we both agreed and we were baptised. Knowing

Jesus makes such a difference. When you have problems, you're not confused as to what god you have to choose to pray to! Isn't that good?

Ginny and David Quay have now moved back to Malaysia, where they attend the Calvary Church in Damansara, near their home. They have two daughters.

— oOo —

"Going to church in uniform was unthinkable, but nobody saw me ..."

The story of Thomas Paulsen

> *Thomas Paulsen, a former East German soldier, arrived in Britain in October 1992 from Berlin to do a course at the London School of Economics. The following month, he was baptised as a Christian at Holy Trinity Brompton. Here he tells what happened to him.*

I was born in a lovely little country called East Germany, of some 16 million people. I had the most wonderful childhood there and when I grew older I realised that we were building up a society that was really new and exciting, and that was what we called Communism. I really wanted to play my part in it, and so I decided to go as a volunteer into the army in 1984. Soldiers were recognised as sort of heroes, in the sense that they would do the dirty work of protecting the country from the Western allies. I thought that was the thing I was called to do.

All the men in my family on my father's side for five generations have been vicars or teachers. My father was the first who wasn't. He became a Communist in the early 1950's. That was why I was not baptised as a baby. My Aunt Renate, the wife of my father's brother, is a Christian. She has two children – Johannes, who is a vicar, and Dorothea, who works in a Christian hostel as a nurse. They didn't try to persuade me because maybe they were afraid they would annoy my parents. I had no idea about the Christian faith.

I went to a barracks to train to be an officer. I made one attempt to visit my cousin when I was in the army. His village lay close to the West German border. Access to these places was very limited. Only close relatives were allowed to visit people living there. I was allowed to because I was in the army. If you go on leave from the army, you get a slip of paper saying everything is all right for you and where you are supposed to go is printed on it. Then they could have control over you. I wrote on this sheet of paper where I was going and the commander of my unit asked me "What does your cousin do?" I said that he was a vicar. He said, "Ugh! What! A vicar! Are you crazy?" I said, "No, why?" "You will never persuade that man about Communism," he said. I said, "Well Comrade Major, I never wanted to. That's not my intention. I just want to visit my cousin. It doesn't matter if he is a vicar or not. He is my cousin and I want to visit him." He said, "No, you can't."

I was so angry that soon afterwards when I was visiting my aunt I went with her to church in uniform. Going to church in uniform was unthinkable, but nobody saw me. The secret service kept an eye on churches and really I was hoping that someone would see me and report me to my Commander. But no-one did. I didn't go to church that time to see Jesus – not a chance. Not at that time.

I got into some problems in the army. It was the time when Perestroika began in the Soviet Union and a lot of new ideas were coming from there. Lots of people thought that we should 'open up' our newspapers as they were doing in the Soviet Union. I still wanted to establish Communism, but not the way it was being done. I disagreed with the methods. I thought our country was on the losers' side.

I left the army in February 1988, with just one year left before becoming an officer. Leaving the army caused more problems for me, because they dismissed me from the Communist party. Personally, that left quite a bit of emptiness behind in me. I went back to the Electric Power Station where I had already completed a training course before going into the army and I started there as an electrician and I worked there for $1^1/2$ years. I was living a very normal life. I was living in a hall of residence for unmarried workers, and every fortnight or so I would go home for the weekend. I wanted to get something out of my life, but there was really nothing happening. I was so empty. There was no sense of life any more.

The months passed. Then in autumn 1989, I left my job with the electricity company and began studying economics at the university in East Berlin. I saw my aunt several times after I left the army. I didn't know then that she was praying for me, but she was. All of them were. She didn't try to persuade me. She just told stories – stories about healing, stories about her life. She was just living out the Christian life in front of me. That was what impressed me.

The real change came in January 1992. I visited my cousin Johannes, who lives in a very little village, and spent a week with him and his family. He is vicar of one of these small village churches. He has got five lovely children – the oldest is 14 and the youngest is four or five. I was impressed by how they managed to live and be happy. His parish spreads over several villages and so he is on the road every day. He spends lots and lots of time throughout the parish and the only time he has for his family are Sunday afternoons and evenings. They see each other for breakfast and in the evening and he prays with them when he takes them to bed. One day he prays with one child, another day with another.

They have no television and play a lot of games together. They have a really lovely garden, apple trees and sheep in the garden. A little paradise really. There are so many children around who are in deep trouble because they don't see their parents very much but my cousin's children are all happy – all of them.

I thought, 'How do they do that? I want to be that way. I want to be as happy as they are. There must be something.' I still had the gap that I mentioned before – the gap in my life. I joined them while they prayed. On Saturday evening they did their prayers all together as a family. I listened to their prayers. After I left them, I was really sad and I began to write them letters which they answered.

I was always thinking about Jesus. By then I knew that it was Jesus who did it in their lives – who did all the amazing things. He was the one who made them happy. But I knew nothing about Jesus. I knew roughly that he was the Saviour but I didn't know for what. I didn't know the story of the Old Testament that people were 'fallen'. I mean all I knew was that my aunt said that Adam and Eve 'fell' and that therefore every man is born with sin in him. I didn't believe that. I thought, 'I'm not a sinner. I am trying to be as good as I can, therefore I cannot be a sinner. There are people I know who do nasty things and they are sinners but not me.'

Also, to accept Jesus you would have to believe in God and that was a really crucial point for me because I was studying Marxism. In Marx's ideas there is no place left for God.

I thought Jesus may have been a very bright boy – like these genius kids who do amazing things at the age of 10. But there was still no place for God.

In August 1992, when my aunt was coming to Berlin to visit some people, she wrote to me to say that she was coming and that we should meet. I said "Yes, so what are we going to do?" She said "Well, go to church" and I said OK. Then she took me into a great church where all the people were dancing. They were singing a song about Jesus giving us the words to shout out his name and giving us feet to dance. I thought 'I want to have this – but surely those people don't want to have me?' I could never look into one of these faces if they knew what I had done.

Communists are now the common devils. If you need somebody to blame for anything, then blame Communists. If there is now any problem in Eastern Germany it is the result of the Communist regime. There is a really nasty hunt for ex Secret Service people. Some of them used to be my friends. If anybody in church knew that I had got friends there – they are still my friends, even now – I thought they would never accept me in that family. 'How could they accept me when Christians always do the right thing?' I thought.

Soon afterwards, I visited my cousin Dorothea and spent three or four days with her in the hostel she was working in. I stayed there as a guest. I told her, "I would love to join your family but I can't." She said, "You can ask Jesus into your heart any time you want to and he will come." and I just said "Hmmm."

After that, in the second week in September, I visited my aunt for a week. By that time she knew that my ears were open and she was firing from all guns on me! She gave me all possible things – New Testament, biographies, newspapers, and all these things – and she said, "Read this, read this!" She is an old aged pensioner so we had loads of time and we went on lots of walks around her town. She lives in a little town in the mountains and it has got a very lovely environment.

We were talking about faith and Christianity and it was then one night that I asked Jesus into my heart. I was going to bed and I closed my eyes and said, "Jesus, please come into my heart." I said this some five times to make sure that he would hear me. I still was not sure. I didn't mention it to my aunt that I had prayed to Jesus. I didn't know if I had done it right. I didn't know anything about praying and maybe she would say, "You can't do that!" I was a bit embarrassed.

Two weeks later I arrived in London. I had applied for a one year's study course – they call it a General Course – at the London School of Economics, a course designed for foreign students.

It is a great and noisy city and I felt very alone. I telephoned Dorothea, who had visited England some five or six years before. She said she knew a vicar in Colchester. She gave me his number and I rang him and told him my story. I asked him if there was anybody in London who could help me. He suggested I contact

Sandy Millar, the vicar of Holy Trinity Brompton, and I went there one Sunday morning.

I didn't know what time the services were so I decided to be there at 10am. There was a man standing at the front desk as I was coming in. He must have seen that I was looking for something because he asked if he could do anything for me. I said "Yes, you can."

I told him I was looking for someone called Sandy Millar who I had been told could help me. He took me into the church and we sat down in one of the pews. The 9am service was over. Then I told him my story and I was crying all the time and he laid his arm around me and listened to me. After all this he told me that he was Sandy Millar.

He took me for breakfast with his family and then to the 11am service where, again, I was crying all the time. I had to ask all my neighbours for tissues. That was so wonderful. I couldn't follow the sermon because I was so shaken. I was just hoping the man would stop speaking soon so that we could sing again. After that, Sandy took me for lunch with his family. In that very moment I felt that I was at home.

Now my aunt and cousins are rejoicing all the time! I have got letters saying, 'Thanks to the Lord' and they are so relieved now. Their work and their prayers weren't in vain. The emptiness is gone, completely gone. I have got Jesus in my heart. What more could I ask for? All my life is completely new!

Thomas Paulsen is now married and living in Berlin. He and his wife Nancy are members of a local church, where they help with the children's work.

"Go, then, to all people everywhere... and I will be with you always..."
Matthew 28:19-20

7

"The light fell on this young boy lying on a bed. His whole face was covered in blood ..."

The story of Sarah de Carvalho

> *Six years ago Sarah Jarman (as she was then) completed Holy Trinity Brompton's Alpha course, during which she gave her life to Jesus Christ. After that, she spent 18 months working with Youth with a Mission among the street children in the slum areas – the favelas – of Rio de Janeiro, Brazil. On her return she told some remarkable stories of God's provision:*

My first day in Rio I was with the street children on my own. It was very early in the morning because they had to leave this house where they were staying at night to go back on the streets during the day. There was a park very nearby. I thought, 'I'd love to take them to the park. I just want them to be children.'

We were walking up the streets and I could see these

commuters looking at me and thinking: 'She's crazy. What is this gringo doing with these street children? They're going to steal from her.' I saw that there were police all around the park and the children weren't allowed to go in. And I prayed and said: "God, please give us time together in the park."

We just walked in and no-one stopped us at all. The park had a pathway and we were walking and singing and dancing. It was a real joy.

What happened next was incredible. They saw some ducks and you know what kids are like. They just started running and chasing the ducks. Suddenly five wardens came towards me and one said: "GET OUT!" And the children started crying – one little boy in particular. He stood there looking up at the man trying to explain that they were only playing with the ducks and weren't going to harm them. And he was crying and I could see that he was saying: "Please leave us alone. For the first time in a long time we are really happy and having a nice time." But the man said, "Get out!"

I was scared because I had never encountered this before. I just knew you had to be careful with authorities, but I could see how the Enemy used authorities against the street children because this man had such a hatred for them. The way he was talking to them was with so much anger. So we started walking out and the children were crying...

Then I heard Jesus's voice say just this: "Sarah, they are only children."

After I heard these words, I turned round and as I did so this man also turned (we had started walking away from each other) and we started walking back towards each other. When I got to him, I just repeated the words that Jesus had said. I said: "They are only children."

And he was totally different. He called over one of the guards and said: "Go with them as they go round the park." So this totally bemused guard escorted us in the park.

* * *

One day I arrived with a friend in a very oppressed area of central Rio by the main train station. It was raining and really dark and this prostitute friend of mine called Rose said, "Sarah, come here, come here." I thought, 'No, what's happened?' And she said, "You have to come, you have to follow me." So I followed her up this alleyway where I'd never been before and it was very dark. She came to this little hut and opened the door and I knew it was going to be bad.

As she opened the door the light fell on this young boy lying on a bed. His whole face was covered in blood. He was a young gangster, 16 years old, and some rival gang-member had taken a knife and stuck it in his neck, his cheek, his nose, and in his forehead – and cut half his ear off. We knew immediately that he had to go to hospital, but he was terrified because he knew the police would kill him. The police kill the children.

We thought we could clean his face, but he needed stitches and we couldn't give him those. Neither of us were nurses. So we cleaned his face and I said to him "Anderson, do you believe that Jesus can heal you?" And he said "Yes, I do. I believe Jesus can heal me." He wasn't a Christian.

We thought: 'What can we do? All we can do is pray.' So we prayed for him, and the power of God came so powerfully into this little wooden hut that Rose started crying – filled with the Holy Spirit – and I knew God had healed this boy. Afterwards Rose asked for prayer as well, saying how she needed to get off the streets.

Four or five days later I saw Anderson again and I couldn't believe it. You couldn't even see where his ear had been cut, and all the flesh from his deep cuts had just risen totally and healed. And he was walking around saying, "Jesus has healed me, Jesus has healed me." He knew.

I felt Jesus say, "Remind him", so a few weeks later I said to him, "I want you to remember that Jesus healed you, and he healed you because he really loves you".

One of his friends had had a knife stuck in his stomach, and one of my friends, a nurse, was cleaning his wounds. And he arrived and said, "Go and ask them to pray for you, because they prayed for me and Jesus healed me."

So you can see how God just wants to show his love.

* * *

Sarah did not return from Brazil on her own. With her was fellow YWAM worker John de Carvalho, a Brazilian to whom she became engaged. Here she tells how God brought them together:

John and I met at a conference in Paraguay. We sat next to each other and started talking about the miracles that God does. As he started talking the Holy Spirit went "BOING!" and I felt Jesus say, "This is your husband, this is your husband." I have never felt this before, and I said, "O Lord, what are you telling me?"

We spent a week together during the conference. He didn't think anything at all from a romance point of view. He just thought, 'This is a really nice girl, really good company and maybe she could do well as one of the members of my crew', because he was going to make a film about the street children.

God said to me, "Just leave him in my hands. I'm going to bring him to Rio." I just had so much peace. I knew he was to be my husband. Sure enough, a month later, his leader was going to come and teach in the favelas, but she broke her foot and so she asked him to come instead. And he came to Rio just the same week that I happened to be at the base. In that week God spoke to us.

A year before, John had had another relationship which had broken up. While talking to God about it, he had said, "Do you want me to get married?" And God had said, "Yes, I want you to get married. I have someone for you." And God gave him a verse – Isaiah 61:3 – that says in English, "At the end of it all they will be called oaks of righteousness, a planting of the Lord for His glory." And 'oaks' in Portuguese is 'carvalhos', which is John's last name.

I didn't know any of this – and he didn't tell me – but one day we'd been praying together and after John had gone off to work, I remained praying with the Lord, and God suddenly spoke to me: "Isaiah 61". So I opened the Bible and I read this verse and I thought, 'This is very nice'. God said to me very clearly, "I want you to give this to John" (I still didn't know what his last name was). He said, "I want you to write to him." I remember thinking, 'I can't! How awful. I've just been with him. I can't write to him'. But I wrote, and I wrote this verse.

The next thing I knew he was on the telephone, saying, "This is incredible." And he told me the story of how God had given him the verse. I thought, 'Praise God.'

We had a lot more confirmations......

* * *

John and Sarah de Carvalho, who were married at Holy Trinity Brompton in 1992, were convinced that God wanted them to set up a farm for the Brazilian street children near the city of Belo Horizonte – but they had no money for such a massive enterprise. Here, Sarah tells how God answered their prayers in an amazing way:

When I was in Rio in 1991, I saw how difficult it was for the children to leave the streets and to go straight to live in a foster house. I saw quite clearly that there needed to be a place in between where they could just become children again – where all the barriers could come down.

Some of the children do have family, but there are a lot of children that have been abandoned. I had on my heart that the ideal place would be a farm, outside the city, with a totally different atmosphere to what they were used to, where they could play lots of sport and work with the land. When John and I got married, I had this very much on my heart.

I didn't say anything to John, because we had other things that were happening. Then, the night before we got married, all my family came together and we prayed. My uncle, David Aikman, had a prophecy for us and it was: "I've chosen you to save the children ..." Then, on our honeymoon, we felt it was right to pray separately and God spoke to me again specifically, "I brought you together to save the children ..." And he spoke again about the farm. After we'd finished praying, I said to John, "What did God say to you?" And he'd said to John exactly what he'd said to me. So from that moment we started praying as a couple with exactly the same idea and vision.

We felt at this time that it was very clear that God

wanted us to start a new organisation, 'Happy Child/Criança Feliz', which would work with the churches, solely concentrating on the street children. So we were faced with a very big challenge because we had no money. We were leaving Youth With A Mission, which had provided us with a tremendous amount of training and security. John had been with them for seven years and I'd been with them for two.

But it was all so clearly from God.

We went back to Brazil at the end of September 1992, with nothing – not even a house. It was a difficult time. We stayed with friends of John's who were Dutch missionaries with an orphanage about two hours from the city of Belo Horizonte. We had specifically felt that God wanted us to start in Belo Horizonte. This couple very kindly told us they had a tiny cottage on the land which hadn't been lived in for many years and suggested we clean it up and live there. I always felt when I was in Rio: "My heart belongs to Jesus, so wherever Jesus is, it's my home." But those words can be quite tough as I found out!

I remember walking into this tiny cottage and crying my eyes out. I can still see John standing on a ladder with a broom brushing the ceiling and all this dust just collapsing around him. It took us three days to clean the place up, but we made it quite sweet and at least we had a base to start from. We spent a lot of time praying.

I remember one time we came together to pray in about November of last year and God said to me, "You're going to have your farm by March." I remember thinking that it had to be me that I was hearing and not God, because how on earth could we possibly get the finance, find the farm and then reconstruct it to take in the numbers of people that we would need? Anyway, we held on to that and we prayed through the project.

Over a period of time we also realised we would need to have a Daycare Centre in the city. It is impossible simply to go out on to the streets and select children to go to a farm. There had to be a point of contact in the city where the children could go. So we needed a house where the children would go during the day for food, medication, a bath, new clothes and also where they could be interviewed. From this point we could build up a relationship and then select the children.

Then, after they'd been at the farm, if they were unable to return to their own families, we felt that God wanted the children to go into a foster home. If you go on to the streets the first thing the children will say is, "I just want a Mummy and a Daddy." So we felt that each foster home would be run by a couple who would foster anywhere between one to eight children depending on their circumstances, and that we would help finance that child – food, education and everything – right through until that child was able to leave the home and start earning a living.

We had nothing. This was just the vision – a three stage project: the Daycare Centre, then a farm, then going into a foster home.

So we wrote it out on paper and started to speak to friends and colleagues and other organisations who work with street children. We also started praying that we'd have opportunities to speak to churches. That was when God spoke to John and said, "You're going to work with two churches specifically – one is the Baptist Central and the other the Lagoinha (which means the 'little lake')." The Lagoinha is the biggest church in Belo Horizonte. It has 5,000 members, but I had never been to it and John had only been a couple of times. So we just waited. We started to look at farms in faith and it was the most demoralising thing. Often they were two or three hours from the city and when you eventually got there – often 10 kilometres down the bumpiest track you could ever imagine – you would find this crumbling house, totally in need of reconstruction. They all needed a considerable amount of money to transform them into places that were suitable to accept children.

We started to think, "Lord, you have to have a place for us!" Then a very good Christian friend of John's, an entrepreneur with a franchise of bakeries, contacted us. He had read our newsletter, in which we had written about our vision. He said to us, "I will finance your first foster home." It just so happened that his brother was the pastor of the Lagoinha church, a man called Pastor Marcio. Pastor Marcio was handed a copy of our project from his brother and he read it and we had lunch together. We found him to be a wonderful man of God with a big heart for the poor. He said to us, "Look, I realise that you aren't the sort of people who would have given up what you've given up unless this was from God. We have two farms which have been converted into camps for our congregation and one of them hasn't been used very much. Why don't you go and have a look and maybe we can lend it to you a couple of times a year?"

The farm was just half an hour from the city! So we drove out – and I remember going through the gates. The drive goes down the mountains through a banana plantation. The farm was obviously once owned by a wealthy businessman who had built a big old mansion-type farmhouse. He had some cows there and a milking shed, and a couple of outhouses for the workers. The church had bought this place 10 years ago and reconstructed it and built other cottages to enable it to house up to 100 people. Everything was white with blue shutters surrounded by mountains and full of fruit trees. A football pitch was already there and rivers, pools and two grass volleyball courts. We walked into the main house and I just knew this place was it! This was the place that God had for us.

John said to me, "This is exactly what I saw when we were praying – a white farm with blue shutters and windows!" I suddenly said, in a fit of emotion, "We've got to go back to Pastor Marcio and ask if we can live here!" John said, "No, we must put it all into God's hands and if this is what God has for us, then Pastor Marcio is going to come to us on all the terms that God has told us, which is literally having it full-time." Anyway it took me a week to pray it off my heart. It was all I could think about! It was so perfect. After one week of praying it off my heart, I forgot about it, and as soon as I'd forgotten it we got a message that Pastor Marcio would like to see us.

So we went in and before we'd sat down in his office, he banged the table and said, "Look I've been thinking, I think you should both move in and make that house your own and use the camp for the children." He said that the church probably used the place about three times a year for three days at a time, so he was sure they could arrange that with us when we didn't have so many children there. And, anyway, the maximum number of children we would take in was 32 and it can sleep over 100. When we heard this news, we sat there with our mouths open! He said, "Move in whenever you like!" So we moved in soon afterwards – in March 1993, which was when God had told us.

At the same time, the other church, the Baptist

Central, gave us their facilities to run the Daycare Centre! John had some friends who went to that church and we started to go there. It turned out that this church had run a Daycare Centre the year before, but it had become demoralising for them because they didn't have anywhere where the children could go afterwards. So they had everything already set up – a kitchen, an area for the children to come and play, and a clinic. But they needed a new team and a new structure. So they asked if they could come into part of our organisation. These were the two churches God had spoken to John about. So it is God. There's no question.

More than 40 former street children have now been cared for at John and Sarah de Carvalho's farm in Belo Horizonte. Around 100 street children pass through their Day-Care Centre each month and two new houses have also been opened in the city centre – one a night hostel for up to 15 boys and the other a home for six teenage boys, all now Christian who have no prospect of returning to their families. Sarah de Cavalho says, "Over the last two years we have seen God's powerful love restore broken, rejected lives and transform these children into whole, accepted and peaceful human beings with a new future."

— oOo —

"I kept on getting this place coming back to my mind –
this Mari Republic. And I thought, 'This is mad ...'"

The story of Roland Durnford-Slater

> *Roland Durnford-Slater has lived in the city of
> Yoshkar-Ola in the Russian Mari Republic since
> late 1993. For 70 years, it was a 'closed city' and
> it is only three years since foreigners were first
> allowed in. The republic, 400 miles east of
> Moscow, is renowned as being the centre of
> paganism in Russia, but the Christian faith is now
> beginning to spread. Here Roland tells the story of
> how he believes God has called him to live there
> and to preach the gospel to the Mari people.*

I was christened at Holy Trinity Brompton and used to
go to the services with my mother. When I was 15 I
got involved with the lads at school and we used to go to
the pubs on Saturday nights and as a result I got quite
drunk. That meant I couldn't get up in time for the
services and I stopped going to church.

On my first day at London University I said to myself,
'I'm going to find out what this Christianity is all about'.
I knew there had to be something in it, because although
there were some people who just went along to church
because they went along to church, there were other
people who were really different. They had a love and a
peace which I wanted. I began going along to a Christian
group every Tuesday. They told me how God loved me
for who I was and that he sent his son to die for me.
Then I went away on a weekend which they organised.

On the Saturday morning, I said to God, "You'll have to show me physically that you exist because I'm not going to be able to believe otherwise." When I said that, the power of God came upon me. I felt physically lifted up and overwhelmed by God's forgiveness. That's the only way to describe it. Within a few days, I freaked out about it. I thought it must be some kind of sect. I had all these doubts come into my mind.

Then I spent what I think were the worst three months of my life. I knew that God was real, but I didn't do anything about it. I felt a deep depression. My mother, who was quite worried about me, asked Sandy and Annette Millar, [*the HTB vicar and his wife*], who she had known for some years, to come round to supper. This was three months after I left the group.

My mother said to me, "You don't have to say hello to them. You can go up by the back stairs. I know you're not particularly fond of being around religious people." I said, "Well, I might as well say 'hello'." So I went in and sat next to Sandy. I think they'd just been talking about me and trying to work out whether it was a cult that I had been involved with. So when I came in, we talked about the most banal things like the weather and how long it took me to get back from university and insignificant things like that.

But I remember looking into Sandy's face. The Bible talks about Jesus 'having compassion on the people' – and I saw that compassion. I forgot about Sandy and I saw the risen Christ in his face. I've never seen it so clearly as then. It was at a time when I felt really worthless. We only spoke for about two minutes. Then I went upstairs to my room and I sobbed before God. I said, "God, was that really you? Do you really accept me as I am? Do you really accept me after what I did?

Do you still love me? If that really was you, then you'll have to find me a church because I'm not going back to that other group."

Then Billy Graham came to town a couple of months later. I had a German friend called Wolfgang staying with me who was a very staunch conservative Catholic – just the kind of person who would not go to Billy Graham. So I said to God, "If that really was you, then you'll have to get Wolfgang to come with me to Billy Graham. Then I will take that as a sign from you." So I plucked up courage and said, "Wolfgang, do you want to come and see Billy Graham?" And he said, "Yeah, I'd love to." So I went to Billy Graham and both Wolfgang and I went to the front at the end. I gave a rededication of my life to God and the guy looking after me said: "Have you been to church before?" And I said, "Yes. When I was younger, I went to a church you probably haven't heard of. It's quite formal and is called Holy Trinity Brompton." And he said, "Oh really? I know somebody there who runs something called an Alpha Course. Maybe you could do the Alpha course?"

I had no idea that Holy Trinity had changed so much. I started to do the Alpha course and I really found my home in HTB. I got involved with a home group and I suppose for the first two years I was just receiving what God was giving me.

I was very hesitant about speaking out. But gradually God healed me inwardly of many of my complexes. About six months before the end of my time at university – where I had been studying Russian – I had absolutely no idea what I was going to do. My main gift was languages – it's quite easy for me to learn languages. I had spent a year in Moscow as part of my course and once wondered if I might live in Russia. But it was quite a lonely time and I said, "God if you're calling me to this in the future, I don't know if I can do it." I was seriously considering going into the oil industry. At university, one of the second subjects I did was Hungarian and as part of my Hungarian course I had studied other related languages. One of them was Mari and I found out that there was a place called the Mari Republic with a capital city called Yoshkar-Ola. I kept on getting this place coming back to my mind – this Mari Republic. And I thought, 'This is mad. I don't know anything about it. I've never been there. I don't know anyone who lives there.'

So I put down a 'fleece' and said, "Lord, you will have to put me in touch with Mari people outside Russia and then what I'll do is this: I'll go there after my exams for *one day* and you'll have to show me where I'm going to work and where I'm going to live on that day. Then I'll go." A little later, I was invited to help translate for a Bible conference in Sweden and while I was there I met a Mari guy. He was translating the Bible into Mari. So that was the first answer to prayer. Then I came back home and immediately went off to the Mari Republic. I stayed with my friends in Moscow, and then on to acquaintances in Kazan, which was about four hours by train from Yoshkar-Ola. It was about a night's ride by train to Kazan and then I went by boat from Kazan to Yoshkar-Ola, a city of around 250,000 people. I went with one other person – a Russian friend from Kazan. I felt a real joy when I got off the boat. There was nothing much to see – just typical Russian dirt tracks and trees – but it just felt right.

The first place I went to was the university to enquire about courses in the Mari language. At the time there were hardly any foreigners there. It had been a closed city for about 70 years because it is where the military factories were. It had only been open to foreigners for 18 months. So I went to the university and enquired about a language course. At that, the man behind the desk said: "Well, we've got a place free for somebody to teach English full time. Would you consider doing that?" I was about to say, "No, thank you very much. I'm not a language teacher" – but I found I just couldn't say the words. Then something clicked inside me that it may be what God wanted for me. I said I would take a bit of time to think about it and I would let them know. As well as the job, they would give me accommodation.

We only spent a day in Yoshkar-Ola and I found that day was an answer to prayer.

I came back and went to *Focus '93* [*HTB's teaching holiday*]. I talked to all my friends about it and prayed. Every day the conviction got stronger and stronger that it was what God wanted for me. And then, while on the beach at *Focus*, I asked Sandy Millar what he thought. He said, "Well, if it's God's will, do it. If it's not, don't do it – because you'll feel miserable otherwise." Then I realised it was just a case of God's will or not God's will. It was quite a simple choice really in the end. I decided to do it.

A week before I left, there was the putsch against Yeltsin and people were shooting on the streets of Moscow. The newspapers were saying that Russia was on the brink of civil war and recommending foreigners not to travel there. I had already bought my ticket and I felt God wanted me to go and I went. I took the train to Yoshkar-Ola. The putsch ended. I got to the Mari Republic and fortunately I met somebody in the train who gave me somewhere to sleep the first night. I went to the university and got a job in a different part of the university than we'd arranged – but I got accommodation. Being a teacher at a university means that you get a lot of doors opened to you. So I got invited to speak at schools and colleges.

I got involved in the Yoshkar-Ola Christian Centre run by an American pastor and his wife, who had come six months beforehand from Texas. The Maris are pagans and have sacrificial altars. It's still part of Europe but they've just been forgotten really. They've never really been reached with the gospel. They didn't even have a Bible in their language. It's being translated at the moment. Mark's and John's Gospels have just come out. After about seven months, I came back for a holiday and to attend *Focus '94*. I returned to find this new move of the Holy Spirit happening – and the power of God fell on me. From my first day back in London, I was really doing some very strange things during the meetings. I was laughing to begin with, but doing some sort of crashing around as well. Then, during the *Focus* week, I started to roar. I roared so much that I found it very difficult to speak, but I knew it was God because God was giving me a new love for him. It was like I had been running away from God for years and I was finally just simply in front of him, looking at him, speaking to him. So I said to God every morning, "Lord, give me your power – I need it. I really need it."

When I got back to the Mari Republic, I was really on fire and the first youth meeting we had I told them about what had happened here and asked the Holy Spirit to come – and the whole place was just filled up with the joy and laughter from God. I have looked for opportunities to go into the villages and preach and evangelise. I've started to re-read the Bible in Russian. I mostly read the Bible in Russian now – and I preach in

David and Deirdre Hurst

John Rajah

Roland Durnford-Slater

Barry and Sandy Meaney, with Ashley (centre)

Ginny Quay

Charlie Mackesy

Derek and Francie Lygo with Freya

Lee Duckett

Patrick and Philippa Pearson Miles

Thomas Paulsen

Richard Daniell

*John and Sarah de Carvalho
with Lucas and Daniel*

Richard Ward

*Karl and Joanna Davies
with Arron and Alex*

Jonathan and Helena Cavan

Robert Taylor

Russian in youth groups as well in the villages. I have cut down on my work at the university in order to help at the Christian Centre. Recently, I went to a Christian conference in Kazan. I prayed all night before my pastor from Yoshkar-Ola was due to speak. He talked and after that the whole place broke out with people completely drunk in the Spirit. The pastor of the Russian church in charge of the meeting couldn't give the notices out any more. Every time he said "In half an hour there's going to be a meal", everybody burst into laughter. He couldn't do it. It was one of these churches that was very strict about order and they hadn't seen anything like that before. God was just pouring out his joy.

I have a great sense of awe for God – his timing, his guidance. I will stay in the Mari Republic indefinitely. I feel really at home there, which in itself is an answer to prayer. I haven't missed England at all!

Roland Durnford-Slater continues to live in the Mari Republic, where he is closely involved with the work of the church in Yoshkar-Ola. He has a vision for Alpha courses to grow throughout the Republic and beyond.

8

"I walked out and went to my room, and I was crying.
It was a very emotional thing ...
total realisation that there was a living God."

The story of Barry and Sandy Meaney

> *Barry and Sandy Meaney were concerned when
> their son Ashley told them he had become a
> Christian. But here Sandy tells the story of how
> their scepticism turned into a life-changing faith of
> their own:*

My first husband and I emigrated from England
about 25 years ago because he had always had a
passion to go to Australia. He was very independent and
just wanted to go and see what he could do out there. I
had some close ties here and did not want to leave. Once
we got there I realised quite soon that we were going
our separate ways. My husband was quite a violent man
and our home life was not very happy. I was in a really
good job and having lots of fun and he was doing

something else and going his way. We were just drifting apart.

There was one other thing. My boss and I had started an affair and, whilst I was drawing apart from my husband, I was getting closer to my boss, whose name was Barry. He too was married although he was hardly ever at home because of his work, which took him all over the world.

Eventually, I left home with our son Ashley, who was about five. I did not know what else to do. That was the beginning of a whole time of great loneliness. Yes, I had friends, but you do not want to involve friends because everybody has their own problems in life. With my family 13,000 miles away, I felt very alone. I didn't tell them anything about the troubles I was having in my marriage. It just never occurred to me to write and say, 'Well, this is happening.' I felt it would have been worrying for them and they could not do anything. I thought I could handle things myself. I was always one of those people who told people I could handle it, but was actually breaking inside. You do not realise it is happening. I did not think about God. I believed in God, but it was really just a flimsy thing. I believed he was out there somewhere. He was remote.

After moving out, Ashley and I lived alone for a short time. Then Barry left home and we all moved into a house together.

His had once been a very strong Catholic marriage. They had five children. But, some years before, Barry had become totally disenchanted with the Catholic church and had stopped going.

After about three years together, Barry's divorce came through and we married. We remained in Australia for a further 12 years before deciding to move to England in

1987. Ashley was about 20 and he got a modelling job with quite a big agency. His modelling career took off and he ended up living in Paris for a while. Then, after about a year, he decided he had lived there long enough and wanted to come back home.

When he came home we both thought he was very quiet. Ashley is not known to be quiet. He said a French friend had bought him a Bible in Paris and that he had become a Christian. When he told us we were shocked. We thought it was a cult. We got really panicky about it. Obviously he sensed this and said to us, 'I would like to explain exactly what has happened to me since I have been in Paris.' So one Saturday evening after dinner Barry and I sat on the settee like two children while Ashley stood and spoke for about three quarters of an hour about his experience and how he felt about God. He actually quoted the Bible to us without opening it, which shocked me.

Here was a boy who at school loved going out on the sportsfield. The teachers used to say to us, 'Oh Ashley is great, but he doesn't want to knuckle down. He wants to be out in the open air.' Now he was quoting the Bible to us without opening it. It was mind-blowing! At the end, we said, 'Thank you for explaining it to us' and carried on with what we wanted to do that evening – but I remember feeling a whole gamut of emotions. We were just so shocked.

We began to notice other changes in him. He was less bombastic. Barry and he used to have long discussions about God and it would get quite heated, but the thing we noticed was that Ashley was so low-key in the argument. He would say, 'Just a minute,' and pause before putting his point. That was not the Ashley we knew. The Ashley we knew would say, 'Oh come on!'

That was an incredible change. It is something that, to this day, we can hardly believe.

Then, one Mother's Day, he asked us if we would like to go to church with him. He had started attending Holy Trinity Brompton. We were definitely not pleased about the invitation. I had always found churches so depressing. But we agreed to go and we both were amazed. People were so normal and so happy to be there. They were all smiling and talking. I had never seen that in a church. I actually enjoyed it.

But we continued to be astounded by how much time Ashley spent in his bedroom reading the Bible. We got very perturbed about it because it was not like him. If he had been a reader, we would have been used to it.

Some time later, Ashley asked if we would come to church again. Barry said to me, 'I don't know about this,' but I said, 'Let's go. It won't hurt just one more time.' He said, 'Okay, if you really want to.' So we went that time. Then we went another time. I think we came three times. Then Ashley started talking to us about going on the Alpha course. We both thought, 'Oh, dear. This is really getting just a bit too intense.'

But he said, 'You need only go the one week. If you don't like it, don't go again.'

We decided to go for it – and I hated it! I felt like a fish out of water. I kept thinking to myself, 'Me in church? This is ridiculous!' When we got home I was very upset for Ashley because when he opened the front door he was so excited to ask us how it had gone. We both said, 'It was okay' and he was so disappointed. I said, 'I don't know about next week.'

For some reason – I can't think why – we did go back the second week and it was a lot better. We actually got involved in our group discussion and we decided to stick with the course. When the time came for the weekend away, I came down badly with a really bad cold. On the Friday morning, I just felt so ill and said to Barry, 'I really can't go.' To me it was not any big deal. If I missed it, I missed it. I said to Barry, 'You go. I'll be fine.' He rang the girl that was going to give us a lift and she was clearly terribly disappointed. Barry told me and I said, 'Look I'll come.'

On the way there, I remember feeling awful and thinking a few times, 'I've just made the silliest mistake.' The next morning, I still felt a bit ghastly, but after the prayers and the talks I was feeling a bit better.

Then during the afternoon, Nicky Gumbel said he was going to pray for the Spirit to come. I remember thinking that this was not going to involve me. He suggested we hold our hands out, which I did. The next thing I knew there were all these tears pouring from my eyes. I didn't have the feeling that I was crying – it was just that there was water pouring out of my eyes.

Inside I just felt this intense emotion. I cannot explain it any other way. I remember Nicky saying, 'Do not worry if tears come.' And I remember thinking, 'Well, that's all right then.' They were really pouring out. It was just incredible. I had this wonderful feeling of elation – and I knew it was God. Even with my flimsy belief, I knew God was good. No evil spirit could make me feel like that. It was just too good.

The next morning when we prayed for gifts I got the gift of tongues. I walked out and went to my room, and I was crying – it was a very emotional thing. I think it was total realisation that there was a living God. It was a slower process for Barry because of his

Catholicism – but he still felt it was an incredible experience.

Consequently, the week we finished the Alpha Course, we started coming to church and the relationship with God just grew from there.

One day at HTB, the person leading the service suggested that if there was anyone who wanted to commit their lives to Christ, they should go to the front. Barry went forward on his own and Ashley and I were absolutely amazed. From then on, he started to change.

My family all thought we had gone barmy. They were surprised when Ashley became so involved, but they were quite knocked out when Barry and I started becoming involved too. Barry and I started to read the Bible and it was quite a hard thing. It was hard to discipline ourselves to read it every day, but we began to manage it. We started to pray quite a lot together, which was something that we really started to love.

I feel God has taught me about pride and how worthless it is – how empty it is. I am not saying mine has all gone, but God has shown me where I can get things wrong. When I look at pride now, it is a horrible thing to have. But I hung on to it for so long. I would say, 'I've got my pride.' God is my total security. When I think of my relationship with him now, I get an incredible joy. I really rely on him for everything. I feel I have to because he has taken my life and turned it around.

He has also brought Barry and me closer and closer to each other. Thinking back now, I find it incredible that God has done so much in our lives considering how our relationship started.

Ashley said to me some time ago that when he

brought us to church for the first time, it was the best Mother's Day gift he ever gave me. And he is not wrong.

Barry and Sandy Meaney are now on the staff of Holy Trinity Brompton. Sandy says "The Lord has done so much in our lives. Many members of our family have commented upon the wonderful changes that have occurred.".

— oOo —

"A man ... looked at me in the underground train
and ... shouted across the crowd,
'Do you realise that Jesus is alive?'"

The story of Sandy Millar (i)

> *Holy Trinity Brompton's vicar Sandy Millar tells how an embarrassing incident on a tube train in 1967, when he was a practising barrister, played a part in changing his life:*

I think I was 27 years old before I heard the gospel in a way I began to understand. I had a perfectly good job. I earned enough money – no lawyer earns a *lot* of money as you know! But I earned enough. What happened was that I was challenged on the underground train in the most embarrassing incident. A man who had just come to know Christ looked at me in the underground train and – in front of everybody – shouted across the crowd, *"Do you realise that Jesus is alive?"*

This was at 20 minutes to nine in the morning somewhere between St James's Park and Westminster. And I was embarrassed ... just embarrassed. And I looked across at him and said: "Er... Yes, I do." And I thought, 'Well that's it.' Most decent people, I thought, would see that that was enough. Not at all. Then the train stopped – you know how it does sometimes – in between stations. And you couldn't hear anything at all except the slight rustling of newspapers.

He looked at me again and I thought, 'Oh no'. And then he said, *"Does that make any difference to your life?"* He said it cheerfully as if nobody else was listening. And they were all listening. They were pretending not to because they were very nice. But although they were looking at their papers, they were looking over their glasses at me.

I knew that they were on my side. There wasn't one of them in the train that wasn't on my side. But I felt they were taking bets amongst themselves as to how I was going to get out of this one. So I said, "Er, yes it does. It does."

The extraordinary thing was that I was hot and I was embarrassed. I think I was blushing for the first time in about five or six years. Mercifully he was going on to the City somewhere and I was getting out at the Temple. So I walked along the platform and went up the stairs. I came out on to the Embankment and I've never been so thankful to be in fresh air before.

Two things really, really worried me about that encounter. One was that I couldn't think of any difference that Jesus actually made in my life at all. The second thing that worried me far more was that I couldn't think why it was necessary to say 'Yes' if I really meant 'No'. Why not just say 'No'?

I couldn't get it out of my head and I went out and bought a new translation of the New Testament. I was working up in Liverpool shortly after that and I took it with me and read it from cover to cover. I recommend anybody who has had some kind of church background to get a different translation of the Bible to the one you're used to and just read it. And I read about Jesus and I think I can honestly say – if that doesn't embarrass anybody – I just fell in love with Jesus.

I discovered for the first time what an astonishing man he is – an extraordinary figure, a leader, a man amongst men.

St Augustine wrote about what he called a spiritual vacuum. 'Our hearts are restless,' he said, 'until they find their rest in God.' And that was what I experienced.

"He listens to my prayers. He listens to me every time I call to him."
Psalm 116:1-2

9

"I stood there in the middle of the airport with all my luggage around me thinking, 'OK, Lord, if you're going to do it, I don't need to worry ...'"

The story of Philippa Savile

Philippa Savile has experienced many remarkable answers to prayer since becoming a Christian. One of the most memorable was the occasion in January 1986 when she found herself at Brussels Airport with the wrong air ticket. Here she recounts what happened:

I was working with the Eastern European Bible Mission in south west Holland and was getting a flight home for my cousin's 21st. The nearest airport was at Antwerp, Belgium, so I travelled to the city centre where I had to get a bus out to Antwerp Airport. I got on to the bus and I thought it was rather strange that the fare for the bus had gone up so much, but when you're dealing in other currencies you don't bother to convert it. I promptly fell asleep.

When we got to the airport, I went to the check-in desk and presented my ticket. That was when the man at the counter informed me that I was at Brussels Airport, 25 miles south of Antwerp. I had caught the wrong bus. He said there was no time to get a taxi between Brussels and Antwerp – and anyway I couldn't afford it. I kept thinking how I'd just blown all my money on this air ticket. I was told I wasn't going to be able to convert it because it was a 'Super Apex' ticket and another would cost £90. My insurance apparently did not cover this situation. I just stood there and said, "Lord help! What do I do?" He said, "My grace is sufficient for you, and my power is made perfect in weakness!"

I heard it totally clearly. There was hardly anyone around at the time, and I just remember standing there in the middle of the airport with all my luggage around me and thinking, "OK, Lord, if you're going to do it, I don't need to worry, so I'll get on and praise you for what you're going to do". I just stood there singing various praise songs. One was "You are my Hiding Place", because when I was going over there in the first place to work for this mission, I was pretty nervous about the whole thing, and I sang it the whole way over on the plane. It has become one of my key songs when I'm nervous about things.

I stood there praising for about 20 minutes and I was very excited. I was really sure that God was going to do something. Then, suddenly a man came up and asked for my ticket. I didn't know what good that was – but I gave it to him. He took it away and it came back with a great red stamp across the middle of it. I asked him what it was, and he said they were going to fly me from Brussels to Antwerp! He said "Grab your bags and run" and pushed me through passport control.

Then over the tannoy it said, "Would Miss Dudgeon [*Philippa's maiden name*] please go to Gate 52, where there's a plane waiting". I went charging down to gate 52 not really knowing what was going to happen. When I got there, I was met by the pilot who took my suitcases and bundled me on to the plane. There was nobody on it except five air hostesses. They said I could sit anywhere on the plane I liked. I had a whole Boeing 737 to myself!

When I sat down in my seat, the pilot said over the loud speaker system: "Good afternoon lady passenger. This is your captain speaking! We will be in the air for seven minutes before landing at Antwerp Airport. Enjoy your flight."

It was amazing. I just sat in my seat praising God. I had heard him so clearly when he said, "My grace is sufficient for you." It was just the Lord saying it. I think there are several reasons why he did it. No-one knew I was flying back for my cousin's 21st. I knew how much it would mean to my family if I was there. It just confirmed to me again that God speaks and he's alive! But the main reason he did it is because he loves me. He is the God who answers prayer.

Philippa Savile is married with four children. She and her husband Keith are members of the congregation at Holy Trinity Brompton.

— oOo —

"Something within me said that the Lord was going to solve this. I had that mixture of anticipation, excitement and terror, because if he didn't I was in deep trouble."

The story of Sandy Millar (ii)

> *Holy Trinity Brompton's vicar Sandy Millar tells of a memorable answer to prayer soon after he became a Christian when he was working as a barrister:*

I hadn't been converted more than about six months when I was due to appear in front of one of the fiercest old-fashioned High Court judges in Birmingham Assizes at 10.30am. I was all set and had worked extremely hard. I'd prepared all that I could and knew that I had to catch the 8.15am train from Euston. At 8.20 I woke up. The situation was so awful that I remember saying to myself, "Now you just stay in bed for at least three minutes while you work out what you're going to do."

I knew if I got out of bed I would panic and everything would go wrong. So I lay in bed and I thought, 'Oh God, what am I going to do?' I had visions of a very promising career disappearing out of the window. Censured by everybody and sent home, I would never be briefed again by those particular people. It was awful. And into my head (responding to my deeply theological prayer which was, 'Oh God, what am I to do?') came this memory: David MacInnes, then Precentor of Birmingham Cathedral, had come down to give a talk in London at the old Chelsea Town Hall and he'd been late. He told me he'd missed the train to

London so he'd decided to drive and he'd driven it in an hour.

I don't know to this day how he did it because I don't believe it's possible, but that was the thought that came into my head and I remember saying, "Well Lord, if you can do it for David, you can do it for me!" So with that I got up and shaved fairly leisurely, got dressed and got into the car. I drove off up to the M1 and I got to the end of the M1 in quite good time although the car was very hard put to keep going. It began to falter once or twice and each time I prayed again – prayed in the Spirit, prayed in English and any language I could get hold of – because it was beginning to dawn on me by then that an hour was quite a short time to get to Birmingham, particularly as I'd never been to Birmingham in my life before.

I got to the outskirts of Birmingham – there's a long, long ordinary road between the end of the motorway and Birmingham, as most of you will know – at about 10.10 by which time my blood was beginning to run cold because I didn't know where the court was and there was nothing but roads! There were roads to the east, to the west, to the north, to the south. I could have gone to Warrington, to Lancaster, I could have gone anywhere, but not a sign saying, "To the Law Courts"!

But something within me said that the Lord was going to solve this. I had that mixture of anticipation, excitement and terror, because if he didn't I was in deep trouble. I stopped at the lights and said, "Oh Lord, now we're here, thank you very much indeed, but Lord I've still got to get to the law courts and it's now 10.10."

As I turned to my right hand side to look out of the window, what should be there but a police car, stationary beside me. So I wound down the window and said,

"Excuse me, I'm terribly sorry. I'm prosecuting at the Assizes at 10.30 (I wanted to make it clear I was on the right side!) and I don't know where I am." So he said, "You'd better follow us." So the flashing light went on, the siren went on, and I followed this car up and over and down and round and everywhere.

At 10.25 he pulled up outside the law courts, got out and came to me and said, "Here we are!" I said, "Well what am I to do now? It's 10.25 and I can't leave my car here." He said, "Give me the keys." So I walked up the stairs of the Assizes and as I got there the usher said to me, "I'm very sorry. I hope you don't mind but we've put in a little application and you won't be on for another 20 minutes." I said, "That's all right!"

One thing it taught me at an early age is that God can do anything.

— o0o —

"I felt a verse coming to me, 'No weapon that is formed against me will prosper'... Immediately he began to roar with laughter ..."

The story of Cameron Collington

> *HTB Youth worker Cameron Collington was praying for a visiting clergyman at the end of a Sunday night service at Holy Trinity in Spring 1995 when he felt God give him a verse for the man. He didn't realise what an impression it was going to make. Here he tells what happened:*

I was on the ministry team looking around as people started coming forward for prayer. I saw this chap with his head bowed and his hands out. I asked his name and laid my hand on his shoulder and began to pray for him. I felt it was right to pray that he might have strength and courage. As I did so, his body seemed to weaken and he slumped to the floor. I knelt down beside him and prayed for him more. He was hunched up and shaking a little. I continued quietly praying with a hand on one of his shoulders.

He managed to tell me that he was a pastor from one of the Home Counties. He had come for some 'refreshment'. I asked if I could keep praying. He said it was fine. I kept on praying and the more I prayed, the more he giggled and his arms were sort of shaking. He was still on the ground and it seemed to be doing a lot of good. I was praying that God would build him up.

Then I just felt a verse coming to me, "No weapon that is fashioned against you will prosper." It comes from Isaiah. I quoted that verse and claimed that promise for this man – that any weapon that was fashioned against him would not prosper. Immediately he began to roar with laughter and I wondered what was happening. As he was laughing, he said, "As I was lying here I was just waiting. I was just saying to myself, 'When is he going to say it? When is he going to say it? When is he going to say the words?'"

He said that during the previous few months he had been prayed for in four different places and this was the fifth time that somebody had quoted that verse from Isaiah. Never once had he mentioned to the person praying what a special verse it had become for him.

I felt very encouraged indeed because the strange thing was that I had felt a little bit below par that night. I had been just hoping that God would use me.

* * *

Some weeks later, a mutual friend gave me the phone number of the pastor and I gave him a ring to see how he was. He had a remarkable story to tell. A week after I had prayed for him, he had gone away on holiday and gone to yet another church. He sat down and heard the preacher announce that he had felt God had told him to abandon the two talks he had prepared for that week and speak on "Spiritual Warfare" instead. It was based on several Bible verses. And the first one? Isaiah 54:17, "No weapon forged against you will prevail."

The next week he found out why this verse was so pertinent. A member of his church tried to dislodge him as leader, leaving him uncertain as to how he should react. He sought advice from various close friends in senior positions of church leadership outside the fellowship. Every one of them told him they believed he should stay on as leader and that he should not allow himself to be knocked off course.

The significance of the promise from Isaiah that had been repeatedly given to him was quickly recognised. The congregation is now rallying behind him again and he has experienced a confidence that he hadn't known before.

The pastor concerned has asked that his name is not used because of the sensitive situation in his home church.

"In times of trouble he will shelter me"
Psalm 27:5

10

"To our surprise, the doctor said, 'I think we should operate soon ...' All of a sudden it was a whirl of tests..."

The story of Bethia Atkinson

> *Adam and Heather Atkinson have both been Christians since their teenage years. But their faith has never been so strongly tested as when their new-born daughter Bethia was found to be seriously ill in December 1994. Here Heather Atkinson tells of their gratitude to God as they were sustained by prayer throughout it all:*

In March 1994 I discovered I was pregnant and I was absolutely overjoyed. It was very much planned and everything was very straightforward up until the last few weeks. Then they found that the baby was breach. We got lots of prayer and they turned her. She was born in December – after 17 hours of labour – by Caesarean section. We called her Bethia, which means 'Daughter of God'. She was quite distressed when she was born but she came out a beautiful little baby and everyone was very pleased with her. It was great.

In the first days she didn't want to eat. This didn't matter for a while, but 18 hours after birth she still hadn't taken any food. You begin to think, 'What is going on?' One midwife, who it later turned out was a Christian, was a great support for the first couple of nights. They gave her a feed by passing a tube down her nose into her stomach. That is not particularly normal at that stage, but they kept on saying that they thought that it was just a problem with mucus. Then we noticed that her breathing, although effective, was very noisy. At first they assumed that this was the mucus, but it soon became apparent that it was perhaps a bit more than that.

Over the first 24 hours it persisted and she was still taking very little to eat and drink. She wouldn't take from the breast at all. She would take from the bottle but very small amounts. The paediatrician saw her and thought that nothing much was wrong. Then another paediatrician saw her and finally we called the paediatrician a third time. The problems seemed to be worst when she was feeding. Her breathing then became particularly laboured. So on the third day she was admitted into the Neo-natal Intensive Care Unit at Chelsea and Westminster Hospital. They thought she probably had an infection and it was as simple as that. But as the days went on they couldn't find any infection. Over the next eight days they were just looking to eliminate possibilities. She still wasn't eating very much. They began to feed her entirely through her nose on the third day but they still didn't really know what was wrong.

For the first six days of her life she was a very unhappy baby. She screamed the whole time. The only thing that she had really experienced in life was people pushing tubes up her nose and sticking needles in her heels and not having the contact with me that she should have had. She had a very rough start, which was hard for us. I remember coming down to the neo-natal unit one day and the nurse just turned to me and said, "Is she always like this?" I had to say, "Yes."

But that night I remembered the verse, "Cast your burdens on to Jesus". And I thought to myself, 'The Bible is sufficient, not just for all things but for all people. It applies to everyone. And if it applies to everyone, it can apply even if you are six days old.' And so I simply prayed that Bethia would learn to cast her burdens on to Jesus, somehow. I didn't know how but I prayed that she would. And – no joking – overnight she was a different child. She became the peaceful baby that she is today.

We also began to pray when we left her at night in her incubator that not only would the angels be around her in that incubator but that the Lord would be mother and father to her, because we felt that we were being deprived of our roles when we were away from her. That was a special prayer for us as well. When she was eight days old they gave her a 'barium swallow' which identified a tightening in her oesophagus. That is when they began to talk about surgery and it was explained to us that it would probably be done in four months' time. So we immediately set everyone about praying because obviously the last thing we wanted was for her to undergo surgery.

The following day she was given an ecocardiogram by a superb doctor who works from the Brompton. He said to me, "I think we have got a vascular ring here. I would like to see her tomorrow morning on my machine back at the Brompton Hospital, which has a better machine." A vascular ring is an abnormal vessel from the main artery which, on this occasion, was growing around the trachea and oesophagus before joining back on to the aorta. It was therefore constraining the two main pipes – breathing and feeding. Hence the link between the two symptoms.

And so that Friday morning, 23rd December, she was taken in the ambulance with Adam and me over to the Brompton. The same doctor scanned her again. To our surprise he said, "I think we should operate soon. We may even be able to do it today." So we reeled, but realised that if we could get it over and done with and if they were confident that they could operate on so small a baby it would be all right. She had been born at 6lb 10oz and had certainly lost quite a lot of weight already.

So they rang theatre and all of a sudden it was a whirl of tests being done on her, signing admission papers and consent forms, literally passing test tubes to the doctors for them to take blood from her, and all sorts of goings on. Before we knew it, Adam was following her down the corridor into the anaesthetic room. It was quite unreal. We had a very strong sense that this was the right thing. We realised immediately that it was a huge mercy that she should be operated on so quickly and that it wouldn't be hanging over us like a big black cloud. So I was very thankful for that. She was operated on by the very same surgeon who 10 years before had operated on Nick and Jane Oundjian's [*HTB home group leaders*] son Tom. The evening before, he had been at their house for dinner. He is one of the top surgeons in the world and did a very successful job on her. She was in the operating theatre for over four hours, but she just bounced back from the operation.

On Christmas Day, I was able to take her out of the incubator and give her a feed, which was of course the most marvellous Christmas present. She was feeding a little bit better then, but they said that it would take time for the cartilage in the oesophagus to strengthen. By this time, many, many people were praying for us. We had put the word around and had prayers up and down the country. My family, who are believers, had churches in Winchester and Wilmslow praying. Our home group were wonderful, visiting us and praying for us.

Bethia did tremendously well. She was in intensive care for a while and then she was transferred on to a paediatric ward and then we were allowed to take her home within five days. She has a whopping great scar, but fortunately it isn't a vertical one and in later years she won't have too much teenage angst. We went home and had a wonderful New Year but we didn't understand why she didn't seem to want to feed. She would sleep and sleep and sleep. When the midwife came to see me on January 3rd she weighed her and said she had lost an awful lot of weight. It just wasn't right. She rang the GP who agreed to see us, but after the midwife left I began to feed Bethia and she went blue. I turned her upside down and rubbed her back hard and she regained her breathing but was very floppy and very white. I'm so glad that Adam's mother was with us and could drive us calmly to the hospital.

We were re-admitted to Chelsea and Westminster and that evening I tried to give her a feed again. Once more she went blue and lost her heartbeat. We are immensely grateful to the staff nurse who was with me. It was quite unusual that she was there, but, praise God, she did all the right things to resuscitate her. We got the heart beat back again, gave her oxygen, but they lost it for 30 seconds which they were concerned about.

During the following seven weeks, she went blue 11 times and at least three times she lost her heartbeat. Every single time I felt completely held by the Holy Spirit. Although it was terrifying I just knew she would be OK. The staff didn't think that. They were very worried. But I was absolutely convinced that the Lord had her safely in his hands. They were prodding and poking, looking for infections and doing tests and so on. Then they arranged for her to have another barium swallow. I was quite concerned by then knowing that she had gone blue twice while she was feeding. I gave her this dreadful stuff to drink and, as they were doing the scanning, lo and behold – she went blue again. That was a very bad episode. It was very nasty, and again her life was saved by the nursing sister who did all the right things. I was praying like mad. It taught them it was pretty certain it was linked to feeding. That worried them and they took her straight back into intensive care where she was fed via an intravenous drip. Even that, we were told, can be risky.

At that stage Sandy Millar [*HTB Vicar*] and Emmy Wilson [*HTB pastoral staff member*] came and anointed Bethia with oil and prayed for her. We really dedicated her to God and specifically prayed for her healing. We took her out of the incubator, which we were allowed to do for half hour stretches in the evenings. Sandy anointed her and prayed for her – the most beautiful prayer – and we felt very strongly the Lord was with us. It was a very special time to say to God, "She is really your child and we commit her to you and we know that your love for her is perfect love and your plan for her is a perfect plan."

After a week or so they passed another nasal gastric

tube and we began to feed her one millilitre an hour for six hours, then two mls an hour, then three mls an hour by the tube, just to see if she could tolerate it in her stomach. Eventually, using a pH study, they found she had Reflux, which affects about 30% of babies to varying extents. In her case, it was quite complicated and she had a lot of tests. All this time we were living a hospital life – Adam was going to work and coming straight to the hospital. I was living and sleeping at the hospital. In the end they worked out medication which controlled her Reflux. They wondered if she might need surgery or that she might be able to grow out of it with the help of medication. Obviously we prayed for the latter and that is what happened, which is tremendous. We brought her home on February 3rd.

We have been taught resuscitation techniques. We've been given special suction tubes which we have located in strategic parts of the house. Her job now is to put on all the weight she lost. She has all sorts of additions to her feeds to help her gain weight and her feeds are thickened as well to help keep them down. They say she will have to be on medication for at least six months, but other than that she is a well, happy baby and they are tremendously pleased with her.

All this has had quite an effect on our spiritual lives. We've been guilty of a lot of lethargy. We've always wanted to have a more dynamic relationship with God and I think this has certainly launched us into that. We've prayed and had answers to prayer, and we've seen answers we didn't expect sometimes – extra little gifts from God that helped us on our way. We found ourselves constantly surrounded by Christians in both hospitals – Christian nurses, other Christian patients and another Christian mum on the opposite side of the ward with her little baby.

What it did for us was to give us a very keen urgency to pray for other people in a way we hadn't done before. We were so aware of people's prayers for us. From day one we have prayed with Bethia and we pray over her every night. That is a particularly special family time.

Bethia Atkinson continues to be troubled by chest infections and in July 1995 she stopped breathing again. Further investigations showed that she is unable to breathe in enough oxygen at night (due to a condition called Tracheomalacia) and as a result she now sleeps wearing a nasal mask attached to a machine. This gently forces filtered air into her lungs and should improve her general health. The Atkinson family remain committed members of Holy Trinity Brompton.

— oOo —

> "I've never felt, 'Why me?' Instead I think 'Why not me?'... I tend to think more of eternity rather than this lifetime."

The story of Patrick Pearson Miles

> *The health of Patrick Pearson Miles has been the subject of numerous prayers since his kidneys began seriously malfunctioning in 1993. Here Patrick describes how the disease has changed his life – and had a major impact upon his Christian faith:*

I always used to be very fit – playing a lot of rugby, basketball, football, cross-country running and all sorts of activities. As a Christian from a young age, I've always prayed and was involved in the Christian Union at school.

The illness started when I was about 17 and in the Lower Sixth at school. I remember getting flu for about three or four days. I thought nothing of it and eventually it went away. Then I noticed swelling in my ankles and lower legs whilst playing basketball and I thought maybe I'd twisted an ankle. I went to see a doctor on a couple of occasions and he said there was nothing wrong with me. Eventually I went to a physiotherapist who took one look at my swollen legs and said, "You need to see a doctor". I went back to the doctor. He took blood and urine samples and I was in hospital a few hours later. This was in January 1983.

I had to lie totally still. They knew it was something to do with the kidneys because I had lost a lot of protein.

They were doing a lot of investigations. I had a biopsy, which means having a long needle put through your back into the kidney to take out some tissue. The unpleasant thing is that you have to be awake and breathe in and hold your breath while they take it out. That wasn't much fun.

I was in various hospitals and ended up in St Thomas's under Dr Norman Jones, renal consultant for the Army, where my father was a Chaplain. They discovered I had Nephrotic Syndrome. They think I got the disease through a throat infection – literally a sore throat. Apparently a bug gets in through the throat and perforates the kidneys. The protein in the blood stream then flows out through the holes. When we were initially told about my illness it was quite a shock. I prayed then and have prayed nearly every day since for healing.

I was put on steroids, which they hoped would destroy the disease and allow the kidneys to repair themselves. This happens in 98% of declared cases but, although I was on steroids for about six months, they didn't work. However, my kidneys continued to work for the next eight years. During that time, I didn't have much energy and regularly felt tired.

Once I reached the Upper Sixth, I played a bit more rugby, but the fluid in my legs meant that when I got cut – which was quite often – the cuts always went septic and never healed very well. So after that it was really the end of sport.

It was in about 1991, when I was working in insurance in the City, that things started to go wrong. I wasn't peeing any more and I had to go into hospital. The protein levels in my blood had dropped too low and it had gone out of balance. I was in hospital for about two weeks and then it was fine for another year. Almost exactly a year later I had to go in again for the same thing. My kidneys were slowly going downhill. My creatinine levels – the measure of how the kidneys get rid of the waste – were rising. The normal level is about 100 and mine was going a steady 300. Eventually it shot up in the matter of a month to 1,000.

I had always said that if my kidneys packed up, I wasn't keen to go on dialysis. I didn't fancy the idea of that. And my mum had always said that if she matched she would want to give a kidney. So it was decided that we would go for a transplant from my mother. We had a number of matching tests. One was not a good match for some reason, another was good and the last one was borderline. So they were slightly apprehensive about doing the transplant. But kidney transplants from live donors have a very good record of working.

In May 1993, my kidneys packed up very quickly and I had to go on to dialysis almost immediately. Six months later, I was beginning to be sick in the mornings. It became obvious that this dialysis wasn't working and the transplant was booked for 5th November 1993. That was an amazing time really. My pastorate put together a prayer rota to cover both Mum and me during the operation and afterwards. We had a Christian Consultant looking in on the operations; the ward Sister was a Christian; and two of the nurses involved with me were Christians as well. These were all things that had been prayed about in our home group. The operation went very well. Mum recovered fairly quickly – apart from hallucinations with drugs – and was out by the end of the week. They had given me very heavy doses of anti-rejection drugs and I wasn't very well for about 12 days. I didn't eat or drink during that time. I was being sick two or three times a day and hallucinating a lot. Most live donor kidneys work almost immediately. For some reason mine didn't work until after three and a half weeks later. However, in answer to prayer, Mum and I were both fit enough for my brother's wedding on 4th December. Things started to get quite good.

We had a great Christmas. I was able to drink fluids and I was beginning to feel full of energy – the kind of energy I could remember from before I was 18. Instead of plodding down to the shops, I felt like running down to the shops. It made a huge difference. Then, at the beginning of February 1994, I noticed I'd stopped peeing. From then on the kidney ceased to work. I was in and out of hospital a lot for the next five months having various tests and endless renal biopsies.

In about May, they made the decision to remove the kidney because it was killing me. They discovered that it was riddled with the original disease, which was extremely unusual. The disease would normally take at least five years if it did come back. Mine took two months. That whole period was really quite difficult and the doctor told me afterwards that in his opinion I nearly died on three different occasions. It was good that he didn't tell me at the time. It was one less thing to worry about. From then on it has been a matter of getting used to a life on dialysis.

We have prayed a lot. Nothing has gone according to plan but, at each stage where it has been very dangerous, we have been brought through. I now have a dialysis machine at home. I do just under six hours dialysis three times a week – on Monday, Wednesday and Friday nights. That seems to be going quite well. I'm feeling better now than I have for a good two or three years, although I've lost a lot of body weight.

A major change in my perspective on God has

happened through all this. My faith has grown enormously. Up to now, I have always been very self-sufficient. Although I had given my life to the Lord, I was quite happily doing things in my own strength because I was able to. I was strong and fit. I have now got to a stage where I really cannot do anything in my own strength. I've had to be brought quite low as a result but I think it's probably the only way that I would have learned. I have noticed that in the darkest times I often have a closeness that I don't notice when things are going well.

I think the prayers of people in this church, at my Mum and Dad's church and prayers from people all over the country and the world, are literally what kept me alive. I can live a reasonably normal life. Some people have been on dialysis for 20 years. It just takes a lot of time and is inconvenient when you go away anywhere. At the moment I think this whole thing has been leading up to a miraculous healing.

I've always believed from day one that I would be healed at some point. Up to now, nothing else has worked: the kidneys didn't work, the original dialysis didn't work... All the times the doctors said, "Normally this would happen", it did not happen to me.

I've now got swollen joints, which normally happens to renal-failure patients after 20 years. It has happened to me after five or six months. We have a strong urge to keep praying. Somebody had a picture of a heavy steel door fitted into a huge wall. Behind the door was water. Every time somebody prayed, more water was added until eventually you could see the door beginning to buckle and eventually it was going to burst open and flood through.

I've never felt, "Why me?" Instead, I think, "Why not

me?" Other people suffer far more than I have. We were never promised a perfect healthy life. But I tend to think more of eternity rather than this lifetime. Thank goodness it is quite short in many ways. I've always thought that there is a purpose in this. I don't know what it is yet and maybe never will.

Patrick Pearson Miles is now co-leading a prayer meeting, specifically aimed at praying for healings and other miracles, at Holy Trinity Brompton where his wife, Philippa, remains a member of staff.

— oOo —

"If you ride in races at between 20 and 30 miles an hour on a horse over fences, people are going to fall and break their backs ... The Lord didn't cause it ... But he made use of the opportunity."

The story of Mike Heaton-Ellis

Mike Heaton-Ellis, a racehorse trainer in Wiltshire, broke his back while riding in a professional steeplechase in 1981. Here he tells how a growing relationship with God following a broken marriage changed his attitude to life:

I always thought I was a Christian because I was a reasonably good guy – I was not too bad. I did go to church sometimes and prayed at times when I was in trouble.

The army paid me through university and I had a good time there. Then, while a young officer in the Royal Artillery, I began riding in races as a jockey. Because I was in the Army, I rode as an amateur, but I had a licence to ride in professional races. After you've ridden a certain number of winners, you can ride against professionals.

At one time, while doing the Commando course down in Plymouth, I started reading the Bible and getting Bible study notes from the church at the barracks. I knew that was where my help could come from. When I was 22, I had a fall in a race at Huntingdon racecourse, just north of Cambridge. It was a normal three-mile handicap steeplechase. My horse fell and another horse jumped on me when I was on the ground and I broke my back. I was in Stoke Mandeville Hospital for 10 months. This was my first real brush with God, because from the very start when I regained consciousness, I felt amazingly in control of the situation. When people told me I was being very strong, I'd say, "Yes I know, God's helping me", because I knew I couldn't do it on my own. I thought I'd been a good Christian guy and he'd been helping me. I had some true Christians who were praying for me. One in particular was Ralph Crathorne, who was my best man when I got married a few years later. My parents became Christians around about that time and asked the church to pray for me.

I was left paralysed from four vertebrae down the back – roughly between the shoulder blades – downwards. Despite this, I had always had enormous ambition to train racehorses, and have my own stable.

At first, after the accident, I didn't have enough cash to start. I had been a happy-go-lucky army officer who enjoyed himself and spent everything he earned. But a few months later, when they realised the paralysis was not just temporary, I received a £100,000 insurance pay-out which gave me the chance to set up my business

I went to Newmarket for two years to work with a breeding organisation and studied bloodlines and so on. Then I met a very nice girl in Ireland, and married her in 1984. But as far as Christianity was concerned I went down a bit of a slippery slope. I was believing in myself, because everyone had told me how wonderful I'd been through the accident, which was wrong because it wasn't me at all. I was also very selfish with big ambition. A few years later, in 1987, my wife left and, looking back on it, she was totally justified. At the time I was working for Sheikh Mohammed al Maktoum – the racehorse owner – in Newmarket. He had about 500 horses round the world in training and 28 different trainers. My job was managing the racehorses, which would entail working with the trainers trying to get the best out of each horse. I did it for three years.

When the marriage split, I was forced to think about everything and realised there was something basically wrong in my life. Ralph Crathorne and his wife then came to stay with me and we started off the weekend talking about how awful it was my wife leaving. Then gradually I came to realise that I was a healthy 50% to blame. By the end of the weekend I just realised I was on the wrong side as far as God was concerned. That Sunday evening I went down to the church that I had got married in and after the service I had supper with the vicar and he told me exactly the same things that Ralph had been telling me all weekend. I thought they must have been in collusion, but they hadn't. It was just the Lord speaking to me. The vicar had given me a fairly basic ABC of how to pray a prayer of commitment to

Jesus and when I went home that Sunday night I prayed it through several times.

It involved admitting I was a sinner, which wasn't very hard; admitting that I was on the wrong side of God; believing that the only way back to God was through Jesus; and asking Jesus to be in my life. Then I knew I had to be someone who was not himself but had Jesus in him. I immediately assumed that having crossed over that bridge – going across to God's side – everything would be perfect.

I thought probably my wife would come back, and I'd probably get up and walk pretty soon. No-one had told me that. I'd just assumed it. Of course that was wrong. But a more miraculous thing happened really. That was the mental healing. The pain was taken away, and particularly the bitterness.

I was going to do an Alpha course at Holy Trinity Brompton but my vicar in Newmarket said he'd teach me himself. So I used to meet him early in the morning once a week, before I went out on the gallops, doing the basics of the Christian faith.

When I left Sheikh Mohammed, I was looking for somewhere to train racehorses. At this time, I realised that I had been putting my ambition before the Lord. Although I said I was a Christian and he was number one, in fact racing and training was bigger. So I said, "OK Lord, if you don't want me to train, show me what you want me to do," and I remember looking in the paper expecting to see a mission going to China or somewhere like that and that they wanted someone in a wheelchair. I knew I would have to respond in some way. Although I was hoping it wouldn't happen, I said to the Lord that I was prepared to do it if nothing else came up. However, the next day the phone rang and that was when I had this wonderful opportunity to come to the Marlborough Downs and train racehorses. So I moved down here in about 1989. I designed and built a very special racing yard, which is owned by an Austrian. I feel I'm in the right place. My relationship with God is brilliant when I get it right. God's in charge of this world and I pray that his influence is spread more and more.

As for my own accident, if you ride in races at between 20 and 30 miles an hour on a horse over fences, people are going to fall and break their backs, and some just break their legs. It happens all the time. The Lord didn't cause it. It's the result of me wanting to do a dangerous sport and I knew the risks. But he made use of the opportunity.

Mike Heaton-Ellis is now in his fourth year as an independent trainer and has been increasingly successful. He attends a church in Marlborough, Wiltshire, where he helps to lead an Alpha course.

> "People will be hungry, but not for bread;
> they will be thirsty, but not for water."
>
> *Amos 8:11*

11

"For some reason I said a prayer, saying,
'Well, if you're there, let me know.'"

The story of Lee Duckett

> *When Mercury Telecommunications engineer Lee
> Duckett came to do a job at Holy Trinity Brompton
> one morning, he didn't realise that it was a visit
> which would change his life. After years of
> depression, he had asked God to reveal himself to
> him – and God did exactly that. Here Lee tells
> what happened.*

I learned a little about Christianity at primary school.
In Assembly once a week they did an Old Testament
or a New Testament story and they got the kids up to act
it. But I just took it as something for kids. When I was
about eighteen years old, I started reading science
fantasy books and they influenced me quite a bit. I used
to read a lot of books involving magic, gods, Arthurian
history and also a lot of occult and New Age books. I

considered myself an atheist although if I had to believe in some form of deity then I had more sympathy towards polytheism, as in the Norse or Greek Gods, as I had read that they had been around longer.

I got involved with the occult after splitting up with my first girlfriend. We had been together four years, had got engaged, bought a flat and lived together for two years. After splitting up I was heartbroken and we had to live in the same flat for six months as we had a negative equity mortgage. We saw each other on and off, in between her boyfriends, for another year and a half. Then she asked if we could get back together. It lasted for about a month. Two weeks later she told me she was getting married to someone else.

I fell into a state of depression. I was trying to get over her and so started searching for things to do. I went to see a medium a couple of times, tried out a ouija board quite a few times and dabbled in magic. After a couple of frightening experiences I stopped the magic. All the time the depression was getting worse; I was starting to close in on myself and couldn't bear to be near people. I also had a lot of thoughts about suicide. I started a course of hypnotherapy and psychoanalysis which lasted about three months consisting of one weekly session. This was extremely hard work but after the complete treatment I felt really good for about a month. Then the depression started coming back.

I had a couple of strange experiences when I tried praying to God. One was when I was in the bath and I started crying. For some reason I said a prayer, saying that I believed God was real, but adding "Well, if you're there let me know".

A few weeks later, in the course of my work, I came to Holy Trinity Brompton. I turned up at about 9.30am and for me it was just another job. I did the work I had to do – which was putting in a new Mercury Smart Box – when I started chatting to the girl at reception. I'd been thinking about buying a Bible and I thought I would just read it as a story. So I was talking to Perry [*a staff member*] at reception (and thought she was nice and everything, you know!) when I said, "What's a good Bible to buy?"

She thought the NIV was probably a good one and then said, "We do this course called Alpha. Would you like to go on it?" At first I thought I wouldn't but we got chatting and she was really nice. I asked her if she went to church and she said, "Yes I go and I'm a Christian. My friends and I are Christians and we have a lot of fun." I couldn't understand what she meant at the time. I couldn't see how being a Christian was fun. She asked me again if I would like to do the course and I said, "OK then".

Being an engineer, I've always been the type that reads the instructions on things first. I like to know what I'm doing. I like to do something in a set sequence. As Perry explained what the course was, I thought, 'At least you've got someone to teach you'. I like being taught things. I like finding things out, but why make it hard for yourself? I like things to be easier and I find it easier if someone's teaching me.

I was going to be away on holiday when the next course came up, so she booked me up for six months later in September. She then gave me a copy of the booklet *Why Jesus?* which I read later. I said the prayer at the end of it but nothing dramatic seemed to happen.

I found myself looking forward to the Alpha course and on the first night I arrived early and sat in my car in the car park for half an hour. I saw all these people going into the church and thought that there was some kind of function on. I thought, 'It's a bit late for a wedding. I wonder what's going on in there?' I was only expecting there to be about 30 people and so was duly shocked when I was taken into the church to see three hundred people who looked normal. I couldn't believe it. It certainly wasn't what I expected. I thought they would be people who would speak funnily and wear pairs of glasses with little bandages on – anorak jobs and stamp collectors. I was really amazed by how young the people were and there were really nice women!

My team leaders were Ashley and Sibs Meaney and I just couldn't believe how at peace Ashley seemed to be. I thought, 'He's got what I'm missing. He's got something I want'. When we started to sing I felt really uncomfortable as though I were back at primary school. But I really enjoyed the talk and the group discussion afterwards and felt really good going home that night.

The next morning I woke up and started to have a wash and a shave. Then I looked in the mirror and this massive grin came across my face and I just started laughing. I was skipping around the house laughing. I didn't know why. I just felt so happy. It was the first time I had smiled, *really* smiled, for about three years. I think with smiles you can tell by the eyes. With customers, I always put on this grin, but it wasn't a smile. My eyes were dead. But this time I smiled with my eyes too.

I bought an NIV Bible that Saturday and started at Matthew. I also started reading *Run Baby Run* by Nicky Cruz. Ashley invited me to church after the second Alpha evening and I felt really honoured to be invited. During that Sunday I spoke to Ashley about myself and my depression. That night the talk at the service was about depression. I stood up for ministry at the end and was prayed for by Ashley and his dad Baz. I felt their hands get really warm and I burst into tears and then felt a warm sensation rushing from my feet upwards, blowing the depression away.

During the following week I thought I was a Christian and tried telling some friends and family, but it was in an apologetic manner. Then over the next few weeks I started to become more at ease and was reading the Bible before going to sleep every night, reading Christian books and going to church on Sundays. One night soon afterwards I was in bed and after reading the Bible I started praying for the Holy Spirit to baptise me. I had been praying for about ten minutes and I felt as though there was a battle going on over me. All of a sudden I started thinking, 'Yea though I walk through the valley of the shadow of death I will fear no evil' and I kept repeating this in my mind. I was really frightened. I then picked up my Bible and everywhere I opened it there were messages of the Lord's love and protection.

The next night I felt really uneasy in my bedroom and didn't sleep very well. The following day I phoned Ashley and told him about what happened. He said that he had been wondering when the Enemy would show up. He told me to get rid of the occult books and pictures in my room and to read Psalm 23 and Ephesians 6. The room did feel better after I had removed a picture and thrown some books away. That Wednesday the topic at Alpha was on evil. I had never felt so uncomfortable in church. I wanted to run. I felt nauseous and angry and wanted to leave immediately, but I did stay.

Then came the Alpha weekend, which was unbelievable. It felt as though we were developing a real fellowship amongst the group and getting closer to the Spirit of God all the time. Nicky asked the Holy Spirit to come and fill us while we were all standing up. He said, "He's working around the room" and I heard and felt a blowing in my left ear. About two minutes later my knees started to buckle and I collapsed into my chair. I received the gift of tongues and at the end of the weekend I was full of joy and love for everyone.

We went to church that night and I was in the front row. I felt the presence of the Spirit all through the service. After the sermon we started to sing a song and I immediately felt God's presence and started to cry. Sandy asked people to come forward for physical healing and I came forward for healing on my back. Sandy then asked the new Alpha people to help heal. A man called Ray came up to me and asked me what I wanted healing for. I said, "My back" and he asked if there was anything else, as my eyes were red from crying. I said "No." A husband and wife named Mike and Di from the Alpha Task Force came to help. I was taken to the side chapel and they started to pray for me. I felt the Spirit start from my feet and 'wash' through my body. I then felt the most unbelievably complete joy and began laughing uncontrollably. When it was all over I felt completely reborn. When I got home I prayed in tongues in the car for half an hour and slept like a log that night.

On the Monday evening I phoned around all my friends, really excited, and told them about the weekend and that I became a Christian. This time I wasn't apologetic! My life has completely changed. I now look at this world through different eyes. I feel love for everyone and an inner peace that I never imagined could exist. Now when I meet people I want to tell them about Jesus and whenever I hear of people like the IRA, although I sometimes think 'Scum', ninety-five per cent of the time I feel sorry for them and think, 'If only they knew Jesus like I am learning to know him'. I am also reading a lot of Christian books and I pray a lot in the car whilst driving.

My mum came to the Alpha supper. For Christmas she bought me a cross and chain which I didn't ask for. So I was really choked up about that because it shows she knows it means a lot to me. My mum and dad are just really pleased. All the family are. They take the mickey a bit. In fact they take the mickey a lot. But I keep inviting them to come. I feel the Spirit's presence almost every day. I obviously have many unanswered questions but just knowing God is enough.

Lee Duckett remains a member of the congregation of Holy Trinity Brompton. He writes, "Jesus has set me free from the prison of depression and healed my broken heart. As I have got closer to God, I feel I am growing into the man God intended. Although life is and can be very hard at times, I have found every promise of God in the Bible to be true. He is faithful."

— oOo —

> "Sitting in my car, I asked Jesus and the Devil to fight
> over me. I said .... 'Tell you what,
> let the best man win.'"

The story of Jonathan Cavan

> *At 29, Jonathan Cavan was a successful salesman
> working for Microsoft – but he knew something
> was missing in his life. His mother, a Christian,
> continued to pray for him. Then, one Sunday in
> September 1991, he walked into Holy Trinity
> Brompton. Here he describes what happened:*

I was very rebellious when I grew up. I was sent away to
school at the age of 14 because of my rebelliousness. I
didn't get on with my father at home. We couldn't even
talk to one another. When I left school, I liked girls and
being very competitive by nature, I thought 'Let's get
good at this', and I did. It involved a lot of promiscuity.

I got good at drugs too. I took cocaine, LSD, speed. I
smoked dope almost every day for two years. I drank a
lot. At one point I used to get drunk every day. I lost my
licence for drinking and driving. I also smoked 20 or 30
cigarettes a day. After I had been living like this for
three or four years, I felt I was dying. I had a vision of a
circle with a dark cloud over it. The circle was divided
into sectors. The whole circle represented my life; the
sectors represented components of my life. The sectors
were sex, alcohol, drugs and tobacco. Then I heard a
voice saying "This is your life. These are all substitutes.
Your life is comprised 100% of substitutes. You have
no life." In the centre of the circle there was a very

small pin-prick of white light. I didn't recognise this as divine intervention.

Later, I learned that my mother had prayed for me at this time while on holiday with my godmother in Israel. They had been in a church in Galilee and when they came out they said simultaneously "I was praying for Jonathan". My mother burst into tears.

It seemed to make a lot of sense to cut out the past and concentrate on work. I worked very, very hard. I felt I had some catching up to do. Looking back on it, God recognised this and he opened the door with Microsoft. I lost all my friends. I just dedicated myself to work and became very successful.

My knowledge of Christianity and the Bible was minimal. I became very involved in astrology. I had a big heavy key ring, engraved with a Scorpio symbol. This was the strongest spiritual influence on my life – the fact that Scorpios are into sex, ambition and power.

I remember driving to my flat one night. Sitting in my car, I asked Jesus and the Devil to fight over me. I said "OK, God, I know you're there, because I've tasted you once or twice. The Devil, I know you're there, too. I think I'm a catch, because you're both after me. Tell you what, let the best man win."

It became apparent very quickly that God wasn't playing. But the Devil was. The Devil was at me all the time at every opportunity. I said "Hey, God, this isn't right. This is an equal opportunity here. You've got as much chance as this guy."

I just heard these words: "I'm here, I'm waiting for you. Just turn to me."* But I carried on and the Devil

---

* Jonathan says, "I had no idea then, but these words from God were very similar to what he says in Revelation 3:20, "Here I am! I stand at the door and knock. If anyone hears my voice and opens the door, I will come in and eat with him, and he with me."

would keep getting at me and God would just sit here calmly saying "I'm ready when you are." Occasionally I'd turn. I didn't know what it was, but I felt this kind of peace. I didn't understand it, so I didn't progress. I kept slipping into the bad stuff.

I lived in Brompton Park Crescent, the other end of Brompton Road in a block of yuppie apartments. The flat used to be owned by Bros., the pop group brothers. I had been at Microsoft for three or four years. I was worth about $650,000. I wasn't any happier. I'd just proved to myself that sex didn't give me satisfaction or peace, nor did drugs, nor did alcohol and nor did money. I was restless. I was searching, searching, searching for the key to life.

One Sunday evening last September I was driving back from my parents' house in Hampton. I drove straight past my flat up the Brompton Road, and I didn't really know why. I thought 'Well, why not? I'm not doing anything else tonight'. I just had this feeling that I wanted to search for this key.

I was on the Old Brompton Road and I saw the Brompton Oratory [*a Catholic church next to Holy Trinity Brompton*]. I thought 'I'll just go for a walk and maybe sit in a church or something'. So I parked my car on a double yellow line with my lights flashing. It was about seven o'clock in the evening. I just walked up a driveway and into Holy Trinity. It was full up. I went upstairs and sat down. Nicky Gumbel was talking. The first thing that struck me was, "Wow, there are a lot of people here." Secondly, "Wow, there are lots of bright faces." Thirdly, "Wow, look at all these young people."

Then I listened to the talk and it just struck me to be very simple and very logical. It was about Tolstoy. He grew up seeking worldly satisfaction. He tried a number of different things including money, power, ambition – and I directly related to those. I thought, 'Hey, this is me, this is me'. He then advertised the Alpha course which had just started. I thought, 'I've got nothing to lose. Maybe this is the key, I don't know.' Ten weeks on the basics of Christianity... I signed up for the Alpha course and came back to the following Sunday service. I went to the same place in the balcony and Sandy Millar issued a challenge to ask people to commit their lives to God. He talked in terms that I could directly relate to about gold medals and silver medals, and winning, and going for it. Silver isn't good enough – it's got to be a commitment.

There I committed myself to Jesus, on that second Sunday. He said, 'If you want to be prayed for, stand up'. There was no-one in my balcony or the opposite balcony standing up. I couldn't see down below, so I felt that I was the only one. But Sandy said a prayer, and I repeated the prayer. I then came along to the Alpha course.

On the Alpha weekend I asked the Holy Spirit to fill me... He did, wave after wave, I was shaking all over. There were tears running down my face and I felt my heart become a lot lighter and true peace come into my heart for the first time in my life. I had not known peace like that. I was radiating for the rest of the weekend. It was obvious to everyone what had happened.

After this, my life, which had been in chaos, started falling into place. For the first time in my life I learned that God was love. I was far more approachable at work. I had time for other people. My boss said, "The last two months you've changed. What's happened?" So I told him. It was like seeing stuff in colour, having been living in black and white.

I was more at peace than ever before. I didn't feel fear or worry. I became more relaxed and lost my uncertainty and doubt. I didn't have any lustful feelings. I believe I have learned faith and to hold back my own will. I am now allowing Jesus' will to shine through me. I have such peace now that I don't have to take decisions alone. They are the Lord's decisions.

Before, at work, I used to assert my will really aggressively and I don't do that any more and the Lord is leading me. I think the Lord wants me to be a bright shining light that these other people can see. I pray now that Jesus' love will radiate through me to everyone I meet during the week.

Often I find myself silently saying, "Jesus, I love you. Jesus, I love you", over and over and over again.

* * *

Here Jonathan Cavan relates a series of unusual experiences as he tried to tell others about his new faith in Jesus Christ:

Soon after the Alpha weekend, I received an invitation to go and work at Microsoft Corporate Head Office in Redmond, Washington, USA.

I was asked to help set up a global programme to deal with large corporations on a worldwide basis. I was chosen because I had nearly four years' experience selling to multi-national corporations from England and had been quite successful.

As a new Christian, I really wanted to subject it before the Lord and make sure that I was really doing what God wanted me to do. So I spent many hours praying about it.

As I was studying the Bible, two verses seemed to

jump off the page at me. The first was, "It is harder for a rich man to enter the Kingdom of Heaven than for a camel to pass through the eye of a needle." The other was, "No prophet is accepted in his home town."

I took this as affirmation that, yes, I should take this job. I felt that I was going to 'shine Jesus' to the executives at Microsoft, where there are a lot of very wealthy people (there are more than 2,000 millionaires in the Microsoft head office alone).

When I got to America, I found that out of 9000 potential offices and 26 buildings on the campus, the office I was given was literally five paces from a guy called Steve Ballmer, Bill Gates' right hand man and a real power-house behind Microsoft. (Bill Gates is the founder and chief executive of Microsoft).

Next to him was a gentleman called John Neilson, who was head of Worldwide Business Strategy. He also happened to be Bill Gates' best friend and was Best Man at his wedding.

So within the first week of me going over there, thinking that I was on a mission to 'shine Jesus' to the executives, I was literally bumping into these guys in the hall every day. We used the same toilets, the same photocopier.... As if that wasn't enough, after a couple of months I moved into an apartment on Lake Washington. I learned later that the previous tenant had been Melinda French, now Melinda Gates (Bill Gates' wife), who I later got to know. These were either incredible coincidences or part of a plan that was bigger than me.

As a new Christian I didn't really know how to share my faith and it scared me to know that the Lord had placed me there, but when this happened I just prayed and felt that perfect peace I had learned to know so well.

I was going to the Vineyard Christian Fellowship church in Seattle and made some very good friends there, including the Pastor and his wife, Ed and Carolyn Cook, but I continued to feel pretty inadequate at sharing Christ. So, as he does, God had to teach me how to witness.

And he did it in quite a remarkable way.

In November of that year – 1992 – I went on a six-week tour of eight countries to do some strategic briefings to corporate customers. I went to Mexico, back to the US, then on to Australia, New Zealand, Hong Kong, Singapore, France, Germany, England and then back to the States.

In Mexico after the presentations I was speaking to the Microsoft senior vice president I was working with – a very nice man – when he said, "Jon, you're English so why are you working in the States? What brought you over to the States?"

And the Holy Spirit convicted me that this was an opportunity to share my faith. I should have said, "I am a Christian and God told me to move to the States." Because that is the truth.

But I didn't say it. I missed it. I gave some career answer.

That evening I was in my hotel room praying and the Lord just convicted me that I had denied him. I promised him that I would never ever ever deny his prompting again. I said, "From tonight I will always obey you whatever you tell me to do."

The very next day I was on the plane flying from Mexico City to Los Angeles. I felt very close to Jesus, and I decided to write a letter to my Dad – for the first time since moving to the States.

So I got out my laptop computer and I started to write

this letter. I had always found it quite hard to communicate with my father, let alone write him an intimate letter, but I felt the words just came from God.

The letter went like this:-

"Dear Dad, At last I am writing to you. I have thought about you almost daily. I have not written because I have known that I could not write without saying something that would challenge your thinking and tug at your heart. However, my words aim to be an encouragement.

"I am playing soccer weekly and play in a team which is doing well; we won our last game 9-1. I have a vitality for life that makes me feel fitter, stronger, happier and more peaceful than ever before. God is restoring the lost years. Many people at Microsoft really do not have a life outside work. The organisation plays an unhealthily central role to their existence.

"By worldly standards this may appear not a bad option... but it is absolutely no comparison to having Jesus Christ as central to one's existence as he is to mine. He lives inside me and he is able to guide every one of my thoughts, words and deeds if I am obedient to his will.

"Do you know how much I craved to speak to you, soft heart to soft heart even during my most rebellious years? For so many years we have communicated mask to mask..."

I hadn't really felt that I had communicated with my father. It was all surface. I didn't get to finish the letter because the Holy Spirit – I remember it so clearly – said to me, "Jon there is a booklet in your jacket pocket. Give it to the man across the aisle sitting next to you."

I had forgotten all about what was in my jacket but I put my hand in my pocket and there was a tract, a little booklet called 'The Four Spiritual Laws' which is the Gospel message in four easy steps.

I remembered the prayer I had made the day before about being obedient and I was horrified. I looked at the man across the aisle, who was a middle aged executive, probably in his late 40s or early 50s, and who looked very stressed.

He had a computer in front of him and was using a telephone. He didn't look as if he wanted to be interrupted at all.

I thought, 'I don't have the guts to talk to him, but I can't sit here.' So I walked to the back of the aeroplane and locked myself in the toilet. I just looked in the mirror and said, "Lord is this really from you? Do you really want me to give this to that man?" And he just said, "Yes".

I said, "OK, but I'm going to ask you again because this could be really embarrassing. Do you really want me to hand this booklet to the man sitting across the aisle?" And instantaneously he said, "Yes".

I thought, 'OK'. I walked back to my seat, sat down and saw this guy had spilled his coffee all over his laptop computer and he was in a real mess. So I turned to him and just asked him how his computer was. He said, "Well I think it is going to be OK." And we started talking.

He said, "Well where are you from?" And I said, "Well I'm English but I work in Seattle for Microsoft ."

"Why did you move from England?"

And I knew this was the question I had denied the very day before. So I said, with a gulp, "Well, I'm a Christian and God told me to come over here." I got it out. And that was all I had to do.

He said, "Really. When did you become a Christian?"

"Just a few months ago."

"What happened?"

And I told him. And for the next hour and a half he couldn't get enough of what I was saying. I told him how my life was transformed when I met Jesus and was filled with the Holy Spirit. He was an executive vice president of an advertising agency in New York. He was having marital problems and was very stressed at work.

He said, "Jon this is exactly what I needed to hear. You don't know how much these words mean to me. You've got no idea."

I said, "Look, I also believe the Holy Spirit told me to give you this booklet. You don't have to read it now, but he told me to give it to you so please just take it and read it at your leisure."

As we stood up at the end of the flight and took our bags out of the overhead lockers, he came up to me again and said, "Jon, I want you to know two things. Number one: God will never ever leave you. Number two: Never be ashamed to share what God has done in your life."

And those were two things I needed to hear. So this man, who wasn't a Christian, had two words for me from God. This encounter turned out to be a mutual blessing.

Some weeks later, I was at home showing my girlfriend Helena (now my wife) how we communicated at Microsoft using e-mail. I took out my laptop computer and composed an electronic mail message.

I wasn't connected to the network so it wasn't going to send. It was just an exercise to demonstrate to her how we communicate. I addressed the electronic mail message to all the general managers in Microsoft worldwide – that's in 55 countries; to all the sales people who look after banks; to all the marketing managers; and to Bill Gates.

I was just showing her how I could send one message simultaneously to hundreds of people at the same time. In the body of the message I just typed some garbled characters.

I also wanted to show her how we could embed a document in the electronic mail message. So I chose a word processing document and embedded it. It was the letter to my Dad that I had written on the plane but hadn't sent, because I hadn't got around to finishing it and wasn't sure if it was right to send it anyway.

So I showed her how we sent e-mail and that was that. I didn't think any more about it.

A month later – April '93 – a girl in my group at work came into my office, needing to use a laptop computer for some work she was doing and I offered her mine. She took it away to her office.

If you have an unsent message, which I had on my computer, a prompt will come up when you turn on, saying, "You have an unsent message. Do you wish to send it? Yes or No?"

She clicked 'Yes', assuming that I had forgotten to send this message – and bang, off it went. I knew nothing about it.

Seconds later my phone rang. It was a friend of mine, who said, "Jon, have you seen the mail that you have just sent?"

I said, "I haven't sent any mail for the last two hours. What is it?"

And he said, "Well it looks like a mistake but you should look at it. It's gone to some very important people..."

And I opened my computer and I looked and saw that

there was a message from me to all these people – about 500.

My first reaction was, "Oh no. I've been trying to do a good job in this position. I've only been here a few months and now I am upsetting all the important people in Microsoft worldwide."

The phone rang again and it was a director friend of mine, saying, "Jon. Have you seen the mail? Why did you send that mail?"

I explained that it was a mistake. He said, "Maybe you should send out an apology to all the people you sent it to."

So I opened up the letter to my Dad and as I read it, I realised how it was just a beautiful testimony of the love of Jesus and how important it would be for all the people in Microsoft to read it.

I felt that somehow it was another example of Jesus showing me how to be obedient to him in witnessing.

The first time I had denied him, the second time I didn't deny him – but this third time just blew my socks off! I thought that maybe my career at Microsoft was over but, hey, I'd lifted up the name of Jesus in the process.

I wrote an apology to everyone, saying sorry and explaining how the error happened.

Just a week before I had discovered that there was a whole group of 300 or 400 Christians at Microsoft communicating through e-mail with each other using a particular code and so I sent it to all of them, saying, "Pray now for every recipient of this e-mail that whoever's desktop it hits, they will be touched by the Holy Spirit."

I realised that God was responsible for this. I was awestruck – although scared of what people might say.

But I had some very interesting responses. A

Microsoft director in Canada sent me a message saying that his father had died three months previously and he'd never seen a son communicate so lovingly to a father. When he'd read my letter he just burst out into tears in his office, uncontrollably, and it was very healing for him.

Another colleague from down the hallway came into my office and re-dedicated his life to Jesus. He'd stopped going to church some time before, but had been really touched by the message.

The president of Microsoft Europe, who looks after all the European countries, sent me a loving note of support. I got messages from about 15 or 20 other people.

Bill Gates himself sent me a message which said simply, "Why did you send this message to all these people?"

I wrote back immediately: "This was a dummy message created to show someone how we use e-mail. It was sent as a mistake by a co-worker."

Then, almost at once, after further thought, I sent another message to him which said, "I am sorry this happened but I've been working for Microsoft for about five years and I want to see Microsoft do wonderful things for people around the world to help them live better lives. That is my motivation for being here and this is my hope and prayer – that your work will touch other people in a positive way."

Now Bill Gates probably gets more than 100 messages a day, so it is unusual for him to respond at once. But within a minute he responded, with a very supportive message, saying, basically, "No big deal. Thank you."

After that, some people would give me funny looks as

if to say, "There's the guy who sent that message..." Other people just treated me with respect that I can't put words to. In fact it was embarrassing as I am basically a very shy person, but I feel the Lord was teaching me, "It's not you. It's me. Just be plugged into me and it will happen." It's so exciting.

Jonathan Cavan has now left Microsoft and is studying for an Open University degree in Biblical and Pastoral Studies at Newbold College, Berkshire. He and his wife Helena have been married for two years.

If you are interested in finding out more about the Christian faith and would like to be put in touch with your nearest Alpha course, please contact:

The Alpha Office, Holy Trinity Brompton,
Brompton Road, London SW7 1JA
Telephone: 0171 581 8255